A Guide to
Salah

M.A.K. Saqib

Published by
Ta-Ha Publishers Ltd.

© Mohammad Abdul Karim Saqib.

First Edition 1983.
Second Edition 1986.

Reprinted February 2004/1425, October 2007, July 2010

Published by:
TaHa Publishers Ltd.
Unit 4, The Windsor Centre
Windsor Grove
West Norwood
LONDON SE27 9NT

Translated by:
Ijaz Begum Saqib.

Researched and Edited by:
Mohammad Abdul Karim Saqib

British Library Cataloguing in Publication Data
A Guide to prayer in Isam. 2nd rev. ed.
1.Prayer (Islam)
I.Saqib, M.A. Karim
297'.43   BP178

ISBN 0 907461 44 1

Printed and Bound by- De-Luxe Printers,
London NW10 7NR.

email: order@deluxeprinters.co.uk

CONTENTS

PREFACE TO SECOND EDITION

Since the first edition of 'A Guide to Prayer in Islam', we have had a large number of requests for this book from U.K. and abroad. With the Grace of Allah within a few months the first edition had finished without contacting any bookseller.

We thank all the Brothers and Sisters who have written in their suggestions and valuable remarks about the book. We are especially grateful to Brother Salah-al-Mulaa from Kuwait for his many helpful ideas and comments.

In this second edition we have tried to make a few more useful additions which we felt were necessary. We hope you benefit from this edition and let us know your views.

Mohammad Abdul Karim Saqib
Birmingham, 15th April 1984

FOREWORD

There are many books dealing with the Subject of Salat in both Arabic and Urdu. Many of these books are well written and provide an informative and comprehensive view of how Salat should be performed according to the teachings of Prophet Muhammad (ﷺ). Unfortunately, there are very few books in English which deal with the subject in the same informative and comprehensive way. The books, which do exist, have three main disadvantages.

Firstly, literature concerning Salat available in English is either so brief that it does not cover essential points in nearly enough detail, or it is so bulky and detailed that it becomes difficult to use it for quick reference, and essential points may get lost in the unnecessary detail.

Secondly, the text of the Salat lacks the quality of direct research from the sunnah of the Prophet Muhammad (ﷺ). There are also books which contain material without any reference to the original sources.

Thirdly, the majority of books have been written according to the views held by certain schools of thought and for this reason some people hesitate to follow them.

Because of these weaknesses in existing literature in English we felt that the need existed to produce a medium sized book on Salat which would approach the subject according to the teachings of the Prophet Muhammad (ﷺ). The Prophet, himself, said,

"Pray as you have seen me praying."

Such a book needs to contain all the essential details of Salat without being too bulky or complicated so that the reader can use it as a point of reference on a journey or at home.

It was also felt that a comprehensive book on Salat in English would be useful for converts to Islam and for Muslim youth brought up in this country. Keeping in mind the needs of our brothers and sisters every effort has been made to produce this book in simple and easy language.

During our research we sometimes found that differences occurred between established practices in various prayer books. In these circumstances we referred to authentic hadiths of the Prophet Muhammad (ﷺ) so that the points could be clarified as much as possible. This was, because, for a true Muslim there is no greater proof for settling arguments than authentic hadiths and practices of Prophet Muhammad (ﷺ).

O you who believe! Obey Allah and obey the Messenger (Muhammad- ﷺ) and those of you who are in authority; and if you have a dispute or disagreement in anything among yourselves, then refer it to Allah and His Messenger if you believe in Allah and the Last Day. Then that is better and more suitable for the final determination.

(Surah Nisa (IV) : 59).

This verse explains about the basic principles and guidelines to deal with disputes and disagreements, amongst the Muslims, if there are any.

We hope that Allah will accept this humble attempt because without His support and help we would never have been able to do this work.

Finally, we ask all our Muslim brothers and sisters to study the text and to strive to pray according to it. If anyone finds anything unacceptable or to be against the sunnah of the Prophet (ﷺ) we would be grateful if they would inform us.

Muhammad Abdul Karim Saqib

NOTES ABOUT THE TRANSLITERATION

The following system has been adopted to represent corresponding sounds of the Arabic Alphabet.

Arabic letter	English Equivalent	Example (Arabic)	Example (English)
ا	a	Allah	Apple
ب	b	bismillah	bat
ت	t	Tirmizi	toy
ث	th	uthman	through
ج	J	Jabir	jug
ح	ḥ	Raheem	heath
خ	kh	Khalifah	no English equivalent
د	d	Darmi	the
ذ	ż	Ażan	this
ر	r	Asr	river
ز	z	zahid	zero
س	s	salām	seen
ش	sh	shuaib	shop
ص	ṣ	ṣalat	sardine
ض	ḍ	wuḍu	no equivalent
ط	ṭ	Ṭahir	no equivalent
ظ	ẓ	Ẓuhr	razor
ع	j̇	Jama'at	no equivalent
غ	gh	Maghrib	no equivalent
ف	f	Fajr	fan
ق	q	Iqamat	queen
ك	k	kitab	keen
ل	l	Jibreel	lean
م	m	Muhammad	moon
ن	n	Nisai	noon
و	w	wuḍu	wallet
ه	h	janazah	high
ء	'		no equivalent

(in the middle of the letter)

| ى | y | | year |

9

The following system has been adopted to represent some of the complex sounds of the Arabic language.

A macron (—) placed on a transcribed Arabic vowel indicates lengthening of the sound of that letter.

Arabic	English Equivalents	Example (Arabic)	Example (English)
ٱ	ā	Allāh	Apple
اِىْ	ee	Raheem	seen
اِ	i	istanja	sit
ء	i or ee		seen
هٖ	hī		he
اُ	u		boot
أُوْ	ū	Dawūd	true
أَوْ	aw		sew
أَوّْ	aww	awwal	shovel
أَىْ	ay		bay
أَىّْ	ayy		age
اِىْ	iyy		

Note: Sometimes an Arabic letter changes sound according to its position in the word; for example, whether it is at the beginning, in the middle or at the end. In such circumstances the Arabic letter has been represented by more than one English equivalent.

Abbreviations

The following abbreviations have been used in this book.

(ﷺ)   SAL-LAL LAHU ALAYHI WA SAL-LAM
       (PEACE AND BLESSING OF ALLAH BE UPON HIM)
R.A.   RADIALLAHU ANHU/ANHA
       (MAY ALLAH BE PLEASED WITH HIM/HER)

10

Chapter   1

BEFORE DOING WUDU

If someone needs to go to the toilet, he should use the toilet and do istanja (washing the private parts) before doing wudu.

ABLUTION

SIWAK (TOOTH-STICK)

It is a good practice to clean the teeth with a tooth-stick, or a tooth-brush before performing wudu. In this way you can avoid many diseases which are caused by unclean teeth.

As mentioned in the hadith Aisha (R.A.) reported Allah's messenger as saying:- "The use of a tooth-stick is a means of purifying the mouth and is pleasing to the Lord as well."

(Ahmad. Darmi, and Nisai.)

Prophet Muhammad (ﷺ) also said:- "If I had not felt that it would be difficult for my people I would have ordered them to use a tooth-stick with every prayer," (that is, before doing each wudu).

(Ahmad, Malik, Nisai, Ibn Khuzaimah)

So, Muslims should always try to fulfil this wish of our Prophet ﷺ

MAKING INTENTION FOR WUDU (NIYAT)

Before starting the actions of wudu it is necessary to make niyat. Make Niyat that the the act of performing wudu is for the purpose of purity only. Niyat should be made in the heart because it is an action of the heart and not of the tongue.

Niyat by words is not approved by Prophet Muhammad ﷺ

Then start the wudu by saying:- Bismillā hir-rahma nir-raheem (In the name of Allah, most gracious, most merciful).

11

ACTIONS FOR PERFORMING ABLUTION

1. Wash the hands up to the wrist making sure that no part of the hands is left dry.
2. Rinse the mouth taking up water with the right hand.
3. Clean the nose: sniff water up from the right palm and then eject water with the left hand.
4. Wash the face, from ear to ear, and forehead to chin making sure that no part of the face is left dry.
5. Then wash the forearms (right forearm first) up to the elbows making sure that no part of them is left dry.
6. Rub the head as follows:-
   Wet your fingers and then wipe your head with them, starting from the forehead, taking them to the nape of the neck and then bring them back to the forehead.
7. Clean the ears by inserting the tips of the index fingers wetted with water into the ears, twist them around the folds of the ears then pass the thumb behind the ears from the bottom, upwards.
8. *Wash the feet (right foot first) up to the ankles making sure that no parts of the feet are left dry, especially in between the toes.

*SPECIAL FACILITIES IN ABLUTION

Rubbing the socks with wet hands instead of washing the feet is allowed, provided that the socks have been put on after performing an ablution, including washing the feet. This is allowed for 24 hours from the time of ablution, and for 3 days if the person is on a journey. After this time the feet must be washed. Similarly, if there is a wound in any part of the body which has to be washed in ablution, and if washing that particular part is likely to cause harm, it is permissible to wipe the dressing of the wound with a wet hand.

HADITH

Mughira bin shu'bah said, "Prophet (ﷺ) performed ablution and wiped over his socks and his sandals."
                              (Ahmad, Tirmizi, Abu Dawūd, and Ibn Majah).
Each detail of ablution has been performed by Prophet Muham-

mad (ﷺ) once, twice or three times (except rubbing of the head and cleaning of the ears, i.e. actions 6 and 7 should only be done once). Since all the above methods meet Prophet (ﷺ)'s approval we can perform ablution by doing the actions once, twice or three times, provided that no part has been left dry.

Amr bin Shuaib, quoting his Father on the authority of his grandfather narrated that Prophet Muhamnmad (ﷺ)'s said, "If anyone performs actions of ablution more than 3 times, he has done wrong, transgressed, and done wickedly."

(Nisai, Ibn Majah)

DU'Ā AT THE END OF ABLUTION

أَشْهَدُ اَنْ لَّاۤ اِلٰهَ اِلَّا اللهُ وَحْدَهٗ لَا شَرِيْكَ لَهٗ وَاَشْهَدُ اَنَّ مُحَمَّدًا عَبْدُهٗ وَرَسُوْلُهٗ. (مسلم)

"Ash hadu an lā ilāha
illal lḥu waḥ dahu lā shareeka lahū
wa ash hadu an-na
Muḥammadan 'abduhū wa
rasuluhu."

اَللّٰهُمَّ اجْعَلْنِيْ مِنَ التَّوَّابِيْنَ وَاجْعَلْنِيْ مِنَ الْمُتَطَهِّرِيْنَ ۝ (ترمذی)

"Allāh hum maj 'alnee minat
taw-wābeen, waj 'alnee minal
muta ṭah-hireen."

"I testify that there is no deity except Allah alone. He is One and has no partner. And I testify that Muhammad (ﷺ) is His servant and messenger." (Muslim)

"O Allah make me among those who are penitent and make me among those who are purified."

(Tirmizi)

TAYAMMUM

In circumstances when water cannot be found, or just enough is available for drinking, or it is injurious to health; in such situations Tayammum (dry ablution) can be performed.

The procedure below is given according to Quran and Hadith.

".....And if you don't find any water, then take clean earth (or sand) and rub it on your face, and hands. Allah does not wish to put you in difficulty, but he wants to make you clean, and to complete His favour unto you, so you should be grateful to Him." (Surah V. verse 6). (The permission to use sand for this purpose is allowed in the Quran).

PROCEDURE

1. Make niyat in the heart.
2. Begin with the name of Allah.
3. Strike both palms of hand on clean sand, dust or anything containing these, e.g. wall or stone, etc. then blow into the palms, pass the palms of both hands over the face once and then rub your right hand with the left palm and left hand with the right palm.

(Bukhari and Muslim).

4. Finish with the same Du'ā as given at the end of ablution.

Note: Other procedures include the forearms and shoulders as well as armpits. These have been transmitted by reputable scholars but the most preferable and authentic is that given above.

Chapter 2

TIME - PLACE - DRESS and - TYPES OF SALAT

1. TIME OF SALAT

Each salat must be offered at or during its proper time. No salat can be offered before its time. There are five obligatory salats in a day.

FAJR PRAYER

The time for Fajr, or the morning prayer, starts at dawn and ends at sunrise.

ẒUHR PRAYER

The time for Ẓuhr, or the early afternoon prayer, starts when the sun begins to decline from its zenith and ends when the size of an object's shadow is equal to the size of the object.

Jabir bin Abdullah (R.A.) narrated, "The Angel Jibreel came to Prophet Muḥammad (ﷺ) and said to him, 'Stand up and pray Zuhr.' So the messenger of Allah (ﷺ) prayed Ẓuhr when the sun had declined from its zenith. Then the Angel Jibreel came again at the time of Asr and said, 'Stand up and Pray Asr.' Then Prophet Muḥammad (ﷺ) prayed Asr when the shadow of everything was equal to itself. Then Jibreel came the next day to Prophet Muḥammad (ﷺ) and said, 'Stand up and pray Ẓuhr.' Then Prophet Muḥammad (ﷺ) prayed Ẓuhr when the shadow of everything was equal to itself. Then Jibreel came again at Asr time and said, 'Stand up and pray Asr.' Then he prayed Asr when the shadow of everything was twice its length ------------

"Then Jibreel said, (after praying 10 prayers with Prophet Muhammad ﷺ , 'The time of prayer is in between these two times."

Ahmad, Nisai, Tirmizi and Bukhari remarked that this is the most authentic hadith giving the times of prayer.

We find that many books on salat state the ending time of the Zuhr prayer and the starting time of the Asr prayer when the shadow of something is twice itself especially the books which are written by the followers of the Hanafi school of thought.

But this contradicts the above hadith as on the first day Jibreel asked Prophet Muhammad (鷺) to pray Asr when the shadow of everything was equal to itself. This means that was the end time of Zuhr prayer. And we already know that all the ulamas of the Muslim Ummah agree unanimously that no prayer can be offered before its time.

Imam Abu Hanifa (Rahmatullah Alai) is reported to have changed his opinion before he passed away, and prayed his Asr prayer according to the time stated in this hadith. His two students, Imam Abu Yusuf and Imam Muhammad, used to give Futwas for the time of Asr prayer according to this hadith, too.

(Futawa Azeeziah, Fatawa Rasheediah)

ASR PRAYER

The time for Asr, or the late afternoon prayer, starts when the shadow of something is equal to itself and ends just before sunset.

It is better to offer the Asr prayer before the sun becomes yellow, because even though it is allowed to offer the prayer at this time the Prophet (鷺) disliked Muslims to delay Asr prayer up to this time. He remarked that the Munafiq (Hyprocrite) offered his prayer at this time.

MAGHRIB PRAYER

The time for Maghrib, or the sunset prayer, starts just after sunset and ends when twilight has disappeared.

ISHA PRAYER

The time for Isha, or the night prayer, starts from the disappearance of twilight and ends just before midnight.

It is preferable to offer this prayer before midnight but it can be offered right up to the break of dawn.

16

Note: — In countries where due to cloudy weather the sun is not always visible it is advisable to follow printed calendars giving the accurate time of each prayer.

FORBIDDEN TIMES OF PRAYER

Uqbah bin Āmir said, "There were three times at which Allah's messenger (ﷺ) used to forbid us to pray or bury our dead.

(i) "When the sun began to rise until it was fully up.

(ii) "When the sun was at its height at midday till it passed the meridian.

(iii) When the sun drew near to setting till it had set."

(MUSLIM)

FORBIDDEN TIMES FOR NAFL PRAYER

(i) Abu Sa'eed al Khudree (R.A.) reported Allah's Messenger (ﷺ) as saying, "No prayer is to be offered after the Fajr prayer until the sun rises, or after the Asr prayer until the sun sets."

(Bukhari & Muslim)

Only nafl prayer is forbidden at these times but a missed fard prayer can be offered. Most of the ulamas of the Muslim Ummah allowed the offering of missed fard prayer after Fajr and Asr because of the following hadith:

Prophet Muhammad (ﷺ) said, "Who has forgotten the prayer he should pray it whenever he remembers it."

(Bukhari & Muslim)

(ii) A nafl prayer cannot be offered once the Iqamat for fard prayer has been said. Abu Hurairah (R.A.) narrated that the Messenger of Allah (ﷺ) said, "When the Iqamat has been said, then, there is no prayer valid (Nafl or sunnat) except the fard prayer for which the Iqamat was said."

(Ahmad & Muslim)

17

It is seen in practice that many people continue with the sunnat prayer even though the Iqamat has been said for the fard prayer especially in the Fajr prayer. They feel that the 2 rakats sunnat of Fajr can only be offered before the fard. This practice is against congregation Philosophy, discipline of Jamā'at, and a clear violation of Hadith. They should offer 2 rakats sunnat of Fajr immediately after the fard or after sunrise. Both ways are authentic and proved from the Prophet (鑿).

Abu Hurairah (R.A.) narrated that the Messenger of Allah (鑿) said that anyone who did not offer 2 rakats sunnat of the Fajr prayer until the sunrise, he should offer them after sunrise.

(Baihaqi).

If a person misses 2 rakats sunnat of the Fajr prayer because the Jamā'at has already started (for the Fajr prayer), he should join the Jamā'at and offer 2 rakats sunnat of the Fajr immediately after the fard of the Fajr.

Qais bin Umar (R.A.) narrated that he went to pray Fajr (in the mosque) and found the Prophet (鑿) praying fard of Fajr, he (Qais bin Umar) did not offer 2 rakats sunnat of Fajr, but joined the fard prayer with the Prophet (鑿). After finishing the fard prayer of the Fajr he stood up and offered 2 rakat sunnat of the Fajr (which he had missed).

Then the Prophet (鑿) came across to him and said, "What kind of prayer was this?"

Qais bin Umar (R.A.) told him everything. So the Prophet (鑿) kept silent and didn't say anything.

(Ahmad, Ibn Khuzaimah, Ibn Hibban, Abu Dawūd, Ibn Majah, Tirmizi).

All the Muslim ulamas, Fuqhas, and Muhadditheen agree with the principle that whenever Prophet Muhammad (鑿) keeps quiet about a matter or an action done in his presence, then it is approved.

18

2. PLACE FOR SALAT

A place or a building which is used for the purpose of worship and prayer is called a masjid (Mosque).

A hadith narrated by Abu Hurairah (R.A.) tells us that the Messenger of Allah (ﷺ) said, ".......... all the earth has been rendered for the Muslims, a mosque (pure and clean), and I am sent to all the universe as a Prophet and the chain of Prophethood has been completed by me (that is, Prophet Muhammad (ﷺ) is the last of the Prophets)."

(Muslim)

This means that wherever a Muslim might be he can offer his prayer, but the reward of a prayer offered in a mosque is far greater than that offered in an ordinary place. The following points should be noted when choosing a place of prayer.

(a) The place should be clean and pure. Salat in a dirty, filthy and impure place such as a rubbish tip, slaughter house, bathing place and a camel pen is forbidden.
(Tirmizi, Ibn Majah, Abd bin Humaid.)

(b) The place should be free from danger. The danger could be because of someone or something which may disturb the worshipper.

(c) A prayer place where the worshipper might hinder movement of others should be avoided, e.g. busy pavements, public roadways, etc.

(d) It is forbidden to pray on the roof of Baitullah (Ka'bah).
(Ibn Majah, Abd bin Humaid.)

(e) It is forbidden to pray on top of or facing towards a grave.
(Ahmad, Muslim)

19

3. DRESS FOR SALAT

MEN

(i)   The dress for the men should be such that it covers them from the navel to the knees, at least.

(ii) The shoulders should not be left uncovered.

(iii) Salat can be prayed in one garment, if it covers the body from the navel to the knees as well as the shoulders.

"None of you must pray in a single garment of which no part comes over the shoulder."

(Bukhari & Muslim)

WOMEN

The dress of the woman should be such that it covers her whole body from head to foot leaving only the face and the hands uncovered. A prayer offered in transparent clothing is not valid. Also tight fitting clothing which shows the shape of the body should be avoided.

4. TYPES OF SALAT

a)   Fard or obligatory Salat.

Fard prayer is an obligatory prayer. Every believer is ordered by Allah to offer five obligatory prayers in a day. Failure to observe any one of the five obligatory prayers is a serious and punishable sin.

The Nafl Prayer can be divided into three categories.

i)   Sunnat Mu'akkadah (compulsory)

These are those which are emphasized by the Holy Prophet

(ﷺ) and offered regularly by him before or after the fard prayer.

ii)   Ghair Mu'akkadah (optional)

These are offered only occasionally by Prophet Muhammad (ﷺ).

iii)   Nafl Prayer (Extra)

This is an extra prayer. There is a reward for praying it and no sin for leaving it. It can be offered at any isolated instance according to the time and capacity of the believer. Prophet Muhammad (ﷺ) encouraged the believers to pray nafl to help make up for any minor omissions or other defects in the obligatory prayer.

5.   NUMBER OF RAKATS FOR THE FIVE OBLIGATORY PRAYERS

i)   **Fajr Prayer**

2 rakats sunnat Mu'akkadah, 2 rakats fard.

ii)   **Zuhr Prayer**

2 or 4 rakats sunnat Mu'akkadah, 4 rakats fard, 2 rakats sunnat Mu'akkadah and an unspecified number of nafl as time and capacity allows.

Ibn Umar (R.A.) said, "I prayed alone with Allah's Messenger (ﷺ) 2 rakats before and 2 rakats after the Zuhr prayer."

(BUKHARI & MUSLIM)

It is a familiar practice to offer 4 rakats sunnat before Zuhr prayer, but this hadith proves that 2 rakats sunnat before the Zuhr prayer is also allowed.

iii)   **Asr Prayer**

2 or 4 rakats sunnat ghair Mu'akkadah, 4 rakats fard. Ali (R.A.) said, "Allah's Messenger (鑿) used to pray 4 rakats before Asr prayer separating them with a salutation......"

(TIRMIZI)

Another hadith narrated by Ali (R.A.) states, "Allah's Messenger (鑿) used to pray two rakats before Asr prayer."
(ABU DAWŪD)

iv)   **Maghrib Prayer**

2 rakats nafl, 3 rakats fard, 2 rakats sunnat Mu'akkadah and an unspecified number of nafl as time and capacity allows.

Abdullah bin Mughaffal reported the Prophet (鑿) as saying, "Pray before the Maghrib prayer," adding when saying it the third time, "This applies to those who wish to do so."

(Bukhari & Muslim)

This was because he did not wish people to treat it as a compulsory sunnat.

2 rakats nafl after sunset and before the Maghrib prayer are allowed for those who wish to pray them. For this the above hadith is a sure proof. However, some people forbid this and others find it very strange if they see a person offer 2 rakats nafl before Maghrib.

v)   **Isha Prayer**

An unspecified number of nafl rakats according to the time and capacity, 4 rakats fard, 2 rakats sunnat Mu'akkadah, unspecified number of nafl as time and capacity allows and 3 witr.

Some people insist very emphatically upon the offering of 4

22

rakats optional sunnat before the Isha prayer but during our entire research we could not find a single proof, any practice or order from Prophet Muhammad (ﷺ) or his companions to justify this claim. Certainly it is allowed to pray nafl while waiting for Jamā'at.

Abdullah bin Mughsil (R.A.) reported that indeed Prophet Muhammad (ﷺ) said that between every 2 azans there is nafl prayer, between every 2 azans there is nafl prayer , adding for the third time for him who wishes to pray.

(Ahmad, Tirmizi, Nisai).

Abdullah bin Zubair (R.A.) also narrated that the Prophet (ﷺ) said that there is not any obligatory prayer unless there are 2 rakat nafl prayer before it.

(Ibn Hibban).

Note: These ahadith prove that 2 rakats of optional or nafl prayer can be offered according to the time and capacity of a person before every fard prayer including maghrib and Isha prayer, and between every azan and Iqamat.

Some people offer 2 rakats nafl after the witr prayer. However, there is an authentic hadith which states that the witr prayer should be offered after all the nafl which a person wishes to pray have been offered.

Ibn Umar (R.A.) reported that the Messenger of Allah (ﷺ) said, "Make witr as the last prayer of your night prayer."

(MISHKAT)

Chapter 3

AZAN ———— IQAMAT

As you know, in all Muslim countries, Azan is called aloud five times a day and you must have heard it. Have you ever wondered how it started?

STORY OF AZAN

A long time ago when the Muslims migrated from Makkah to Madinah they used to agree about a fixed time for the congregational prayer. They found it difficult to remember the time fixed for the prayer sometimes, especially when they were busy doing their work. One day Prophet Muhammad (🕌) and the Muslims discussed the matter of calling the people for the congregational prayer at the exact time. Some of the believers suggested the use of something like the bell of the Christians, others suggested the use of a horn like that of the Jews, but Umar (R.A.) suggested sending someone to announce the prayer. Then Allah's Messenger (🕌) appointed Bilal to call the people to prayer. But it seems through the study of ahadith that the method was not satisfactory. Then Prophet Muhammad (🕌) agreed to use a Naqoose (a conch), something like the bell of the Christians but he was not happy to use it because of its similarity with the Christians.

After Prophet Muhammad (🕌) had ordered a bell to be made so that it could be struck to gather the people to prayer; on that same day a companion, Abdullah bin Zaid bin Abd Rabbihi, said, "I was sleeping when I saw a man carrying a naqoose in his hands, and I said, 'Servant of Allah, will you sell this to me?' When he asked what I would do with it? I replied, that we would use it to call the people to prayer. He said, 'Shall I not guide you to something better than that?' I replied, 'Certainly,' so he told me to say,

'Allāhu Akbar, Allāhu Akbar, Allāhu Akbar, Allāhu Akbar, Ash hadu al lā ilāha illal lāh, ash hadu al lāilāha illal lāh, Ash hadu an-na Muḥammadar rasūlul-lāh, Ash hadu an-na Muḥammadar rasūlul-,lāh, hayya 'alas salāh, hayya 'alas salāh, hayya 'alal falāh, hayya 'alal-falāh, Allāhu Akbar, Allāhu Akbar, Lā ilāha illal lāh.'

"After the Azan the stranger kept quiet for a while and then said, 'When the congregation is ready you should say:- Allāhu Akbar, Allāhu Akbar, Ash hadu al lā ilāha illal lāh, Ash hadu an- an Muhammadar rasūlul-lāh, hayya 'alas salāh, hayya 'alal falāh, qad qāma tis salāh, qad qāma tis salāh , Allāhu Akbar, Allāhu Akbar, lā ilāha illal lāh.'

"When I told Allah's Messenger (ﷺ) in the morning what I had seen, he said, 'It is a true vision, insha-Allah, so get up along with Bilal, and when you have taught him what you have seen let him use it in making the call to prayer, for he has stronger voice than you have.'

"So I got up along with Bilal and began to teach it to him, and he used it in making the call to prayer.

"Umar bin al-Khattab heard this when he was in his house, and he came out trailing his cloak and said, 'Messenger of Allah (ﷺ), by Him who has sent you with the truth, I have seen the same kind of thing as has been revealed.' To this Allah's Messenger (ﷺ) replied, 'Praise be to Allah!'"

(Darmi, Ahmad, Ibn Majah, Ibn, Khuzaimah, Tirmizi)

So from that day on to the present day Azan is said to gather the people for the congregational prayer.

THE MUAZZIN

A person who calls people for the congregational prayer is called a Muazzin. Before saying the Azan he should stand facing Ka'bah in Makkah. He should raise his hands to his ears putting the tips of forefingers into his ears and call in a loud voice. When he says Hayya 'alas Salāh he should turn his face to the right and when he says Hayya 'alal Falāh he should turn his face to the left.

TEXT OF THE AZAN

Allāhu Akbar
Allah is the greatest
Allāhu Akbar
Allah is the greatest
Allāhu Akbar
Allah is the greatest
Allāhu Akbar
Allah is the greatest
Ash hadu al lā ilāha illal lāh
I bear witness that there is no deity but Allah
Ash hadu al lā ilāha illal lāh
I bear witness that there is no deity but Allah
Ash hadu an-an Muḥammadar rasūlul lāh
I bear witness that Muhammad (ﷺ) is the messenger of Allah.
Ash hadu an-an Muḥammadar rasūlul lāh
I bear witness that Muhammad (ﷺ) is the messenger of Allah.
Hayya 'alas salāh
Come to Prayer
Hayya 'alas salāh
Come to Prayer
Hayya 'alal falāh
Come to your Good
Hayya 'alal falāh
Come to your Good
Allāhu Akbar
Allah is the greatest
Allāhu Akbar
Allah is the greatest
Lā ilāha illal lāh
There is no deity but Allah

AZAN FOR FAJR

An additional phrase is included in the Azan for the Fajr prayer after the second Hayya 'alal Falāh.

26

$$\text{اَلصَّلٰوةُ خَيْرٌ مِّنَ النَّوْمِ}$$

$$\text{اَلصَّلٰوةُ خَيْرٌ مِّنَ النَّوْمِ}$$

Assalatū Kḥayrum minan nawm - Prayer is better than sleep.
Assalatū kḥayrum minan nawm - Prayer is better than sleep.

LISTENING TO THE AZAN

1) When the believers hear the Azan they should listen to it in silence and repeat each phrase of the Azan in silence immediately after the Muazzin has finished saying the phrase.

2) When the Muazzin says:- Hayya 'alas salāh and Hayya 'alal falāh - the listener should say in reply:- Lahawla walā quwwata illā Bil-lāh.

$$\text{لَاحَوْلَ وَلَاقُوَّةَ اِلَّا بِاللَّهِ}$$

3) When the Aẓan has been completed, the listener and **the** Muazzin recite Darūd unto Prophet Muḥammad (ﷺ) followed by Du'ā.

DARŪD AFTER THE AZAN

$$\text{اَللّٰهُمَّ صَلِّ عَلٰى مُحَمَّدٍ وَّعَلٰى اٰلِ مُحَمَّدٍ كَمَا صَلَّيْتَ عَلٰى}$$
$$\text{اِبْرَاهِيْمَ وَعَلٰى اٰلِ اِبْرَاهِيْمَ اِنَّكَ حَمِيْدٌ مَّجِيْدٌ ﮩ اَللّٰهُمَّ}$$
$$\text{بَارِكْ عَلٰى مُحَمَّدٍ وَّعَلٰى اٰلِ مُحَمَّدٍ كَمَا بَارَكْتَ عَلٰى اِبْرَاهِيْمَ}$$
$$\text{وَعَلٰى اٰلِ اِبْرَاهِيْمَ اِنَّكَ حَمِيْدٌ مَّجِيْدٌ ﮩ}$$

"Allāh humma sal-li 'alā Muḥammadin wa 'alā ali Muḥammadin

kamā sal-la,ta 'alā Ibrāheema wa 'alā āli Ibrāheema innaka hameedum majeed."

"Oh Allah, let your peace come upon Muhammad (ﷺ) as you have sent peace upon Ibrahim (A.S.) and his family. Truly you are praiseworthy and glorious."

"Allāh humma bārik 'alā Muhammadin wa 'alā ali Muhammadin kamā bārakta 'alā Ibrāheema wa 'alā āli Ibrāheema innaka hameedum majeed."

"Oh, Allah, bless Muhammad (ﷺ) and the family of Muhammad (ﷺ) as you have blessed Ibrahim (A.S.) and his family. Truly you are praiseworthy and glorious."

DU'Ā OF AZAN

اَللّٰهُمَّ رَبِّ هٰذِهِ الدَّعْوَةِ التَّآمَّةِ وَالصَّلوٰةِ الْقَآئِكَمَةِ
اٰتِ مُحَمَّدَ ۨ الْوَسِيْلَةَ وَالْفَضِيْلَةَ وَابْعَثْهُ مَقَامًا مَحْمُوْدَ
ۨالَّذِیْ وَعَدْ تَهُ ۥ

*"Allāh humma rabba
Hāżi hid da'wa tit
tām mati was salā
til Qā imati āti
Muhammada nil waseelata
wal Fadeelata wab 'ath-hu
maǧamam mahmūda nil
lazee wa ad tahū."*

"Oh Allah! Lord of this complete prayer of ours. By the blessing of it, give Muhammad (ﷺ) his eternal rights of intercession, distinction and highest class (in paradise). And raise him to the promised rank you have promised him.

Jabir (R.A.) reported Allah's Messenger (ﷺ) as saying, "If anyone says when he hears the Azan, 'Oh God, Lord of this

28

perfect call and of the prayer which is established for all time, grant Muhammad (ﷺ) the Wasila and excellency, and raise him up in a praiseworthy position which you have promised,' he will be assured of my intercession."

(Bukhari)

IQAMAT

Iqamat is the second call to prayer and is uttered immediately before the beginning of the obligatory prayer offered with congregation.

TEXT OF IQAMAT

اَللّٰهُ اَكْبَرُ اَللّٰهُ اَكْبَرُ ۞

اَشْهَدُ اَنْ لَآ اِلٰهَ اِلَّا اللّٰهُ ۞

اَشْهَدُ اَنَّ مُحَمَّدًا رَّسُوْلُ اللّٰهِ ۞

حَيَّ عَلَى الصَّلٰوةِ ۞ حَيَّ عَلَى الْفَلَاحِ ۞

قَدْ قَامَتِ الصَّلٰوةُ ۞ قَدْ قَامَتِ الصَّلٰوةُ ۞

اَللّٰهُ اَكْبَرُ اَللّٰهُ اَكْبَرُ لَآ اِلٰهَ اِلَّا اللّٰهُ ۞

Allāhu Akbar
Allah is the greatest
Allāhu Akbar
Allah is the greatest
Ash hadu an lā ilāha illal lāh
I bear witness that there is no deity but Allah.
Ash hādu anna Muhammadar rasūlul lāh
I bear witness that Muhammad (ﷺ) is the messenger of Allah.
Hayya 'alas Salāh
Come to Prayer.
Hayya 'alal falāh
Come to your good.
Qad qāmatis salāh
Jamā'at is ready.
Qad qāmatis salāh
Jamā'at is ready.

29

Allāh Akbar
Allah is the Greatest.
Allāh Akbar
Allah is the Greatest.
Lā ilāha illal lāḥ
There is no deity but Allah.

This text of Iqamat is the same as that mentioned in the hadith of Abdullah bin Zaid bin Abd Rabbihi who was the first to have the vision about Aẓan.

Chapter 4

CONDUCT OF SALAT (PRAYER)

SUTRA

Before a person starts to pray he should place something a short distance in front of him of the place where he prostrates (does Sajdah). Such an object is called SUTRA and is used when the person is praying alone. A person passing in front of the person in prayer, should pass on the outside of the sutra.

If someone is praying in congregation, then the imam acts as the sutra. The imam, however, must have his own individual sutra in front of him.

QIBLAH

Wherever a person is in the world, he should face towards the Ka'bah when he is going to pray. The Ka'bah is in the sacred mosque of Makkah in Saudi Arabia. Facing towards Qiblah (Ka'bah) is a very important condition of performance of prayer. However, if the person is in a place such as a desert, jungle, unknown strange city or a place where he does not know the direction of the Qiblah, he should try his best to find out the direction of Qiblah from others. However, if it is not possible then he should use his judgement and face in a direction which he thinks is that of Qiblah and Allah will accept his prayer.

It is important for a person to start the prayer facing the direction of Qiblah and it does not matter if his direction changes while he is praying, e.g. in a ship, a train or an aeroplane, etc.

NOTE: Nowadays, a compass is available which gives the direction of Qiblah. In strange places and aeroplanes it is a useful instrument to possess.

INTENTION

After facing the Qiblah the person should make niyat (intention). The intention is made within his mind, so the person should think about the particular obligatory, optional or nafl prayer he intends to perform. He should not utter the words of niyat aloud, as this is not authentic or approved by the Prophet (鬱).

TAKBEER TAHRIMAH

After making niyat the person should start his prayer saying "Allāhu akbar" (Allah is the greatest) raising both of his hands to the shoulders, with fingers stretching to the earlobes. He should then fold his hands over his chest right hand over the left hand. This first "Allāhu Akbar" is called Takbeer Tahrimah because after saying Takbeer every common and worldly action, talk or movement is forbidden. Throughout the prayer the eyes of the worshipper should point to the spot where the forehead rests in Sajdah.

WHERE SHOULD THE HANDS BE FOLDED AND PLACED AFTER SAYING TAKBEER TAHRIMAH?

Some people place their hands under the navel, others place them under the chest but there are hadiths which state that Prophet Muhammad (鬱) used to place his hands over his chest.

a) Halb Ataee (R.A.)*reported:* "I saw the Prophet (鬱) placing his right hand over his left hand over his chest."

(Ahmad, Tirmizi).

b) Wāil b. Hajr (R.A.) said: "I prayed with Prophet Muhammad (鬱) and he put his right hand over his left hand over his chest." (Ibn Khuzaimah, Abu Dawūd, Muslim).

There are some other narrations which state that some Fuqha used to place their hands under the chest but above the navel.

Placing the hands in either of these positions is correct but it is better to place them over the chest according to the practice of Prophet Muhammad (鬱) as mentioned in the above authentic hadiths.

RECITATION BEFORE FATIHAH

There are several duās which Prophet Muhammad (ﷺ)
used to recite before Fatihah. We will mention two of them.

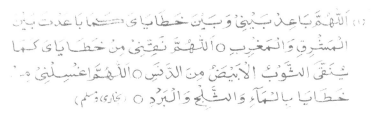

*"Allāh humma bā'id baynee wa bayna khatāyāya Kamā bā'adta
baynal mashriqi wal maghribi, Allāh humma naq-qinee min
khatāyāya kamā yunaq-qath thawbul abyadu minad danasi, Allāh
hum maghsilnee min Khatāyāya bil māee wath thalji wal bardi."*

"O Allah set me apart from my sins as East and West are apart
from each other.
"O Allah, cleanse me from my sins as a white garment is cleansed
from dirt after thorough washing.
"O Allah, wash me off from my sins with water, snow and hail."
(Buknari and Muslim).

If a person does not know the du'ā just mentioned then he should
recite the following one. Umar (R.A.) is reported to nave used this
du'ā after saying Takbeer Tahrimah.

*"Subhāna Kallāh humma wabi hamdika watabāra kasmuka wata
'ālā jad-duka walā ilāha ghayruk."*

"Glory be to you, O Allah, and all praises are due unto you, and
blessed is your name and high is your majesty and none is worthy
of worship but you."

A person can read both du'ās, together or just one of them or any of the other du'ās which are approved by Prophet Muhammad (ﷺ) and, there are about 7. These du'ās can be found in different places of several Books of Hadith, e.g. Muslim, Tirmizi, Musnad-e-Imam Ahmad, Abu Dawūd, Darqutni, Nisai, Ibn Majah, Ibn Hibban, Muatta Imam Malik).

All of the 7 du'ās can be read together before reciting surah Fatihah.

This recitation is called Du'ā-ul-Istiftah which means Du'ā of starting. Du'ā-ul-Istiftah should only be recited in the first rakat.

TA'AWWUZ

Then the person who is praying should say:-

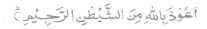

"A'ūżu bil-lāhi minash Shaytā nir-rajeem."

"I seek Allah's protection from satan who is accursed."
This should only be said in the first rakat.

TASMIAH

Then the person who is praying should say:

"Bismillāh hir-rahmā nir-raheem."

"In the name of Allah, the most kind and the most merciful."
This should be said in every rakat before reciting surah Fatihah.

SURAH FATIHAH

Then the person praying should recite surah Fatihah.

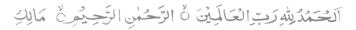

34

يَوْمِ الدِّيْنِ ٥ اِيَّاكَ نَعْبُدُ وَ اِيَّاكَ نَسْتَعِيْنُ ٥ اِهْدِنَا
الصِّرَاطَ الْمُسْتَقِيْمَ ٥ صِرَاطَ الَّذِيْنَ اَنْعَمْتَ عَلَيْهِمْ
غَيْرِ الْمَغْضُوْبِ عَلَيْهِمْ وَلَا الضَّالِّيْنَ ٥ اٰمين ـ

"Alḥamdu lil-lāhi rab-bil 'ālameen.
Ar raḥmā nir-raḥeem.
Māliki yawmid - deen
Iyyāka na'budu wa
iyyāka nasta'een.
ihdinaṣ sirātal mustaqeem.
Ṣirāṭal laẓeena an'amta 'alayhim.
Ghayril maghdūbi
'alayhim walaḍ ḍāl-leen, Ameen."

"Praise is only for Allah, Lord
of the Universe.
The most kind, the most merciful.
The master of the Day of Judgement.
You alone we worship and to you alone
we pray for help.
Show us the straight way,
the way of those whom you have blessed.
Who have not deserved your anger,
Nor gone astray."

Reciting Fatihah is so important that Prophet Muhammad
ﷺ said that no prayer was acceptable without the recitation of Fatihah.

a) Ubadah bin Samit (R.A.) reported Allah's Messenger
(ﷺ) as saying: "There is no prayer acceptable without
reciting Surah Fatihah." (Bukhari Muslim, Ahmad, Abu
Dawūd, Tirmizi, Nisai, Ibn Majah).

b) Abu Hurairah (R.A.) reported that the Messenger of Allah
(ﷺ) was saying that anyone who prayed any kind of prayer
and did not read in that Ummul Quran, and in one version
Fatihah-tul-Kitab, his prayer will be deficient, will be deficient,

35

will be deficient, and not complete. (Bukhari, Muslim, Ahmad).

c) Abu Hurairah (R.A.) reported Allah's Messenger (ﷺ) as saying: "No prayer will benefit a person who did not read in that, surah Fatihah." (Ibn Khuzaimah, Ibn Hibban, Ahmad).

In the light of the above hadiths we understand that Surah Fatihah must be recited or read in every rakat of any type of prayer.

RECITATION OF SURAH FATIHAH BEHIND AN IMAM.

Some people are very confused whether they should or should not read Surah Fatihah while praying in congregation. But there should not be any confusion in this matter as the following hadith very clearly answers the question.

a) Ubadah bin Samit (R.A.) said: "We were behind the Prophet (ﷺ) in the Fajr prayer, and he recited a passage from the Quran, but the recitation became difficult for him. Then when he finished he said, 'Do you recite behind your Imam?' We replied, 'Yes, Messenger of Allah (ﷺ) .' Then the Messenger of Allah (ﷺ) said: 'Do not recite anything (behind the Imam) except Fatihah-tul-Kitab (Surah Fatihah) because he who does not include it in his recitation in prayer his prayer is not valid.'" (Abu Dawūd, Tirmizi).

b) Abu Hurairah (R.A.) reported that the Messenger of Allah (ﷺ) said: "If anyone observes prayer (salat) in which he does not read Ummul Qurān (Fatihah), it is deficient, it is deficient, it is deficient, and not complete." It was said to Abu Hurairah: "What should we do when we are behind an Imam?" He, (Abu Hurairah) (R.A.) replied, "Read it in silence....." (Muslim).

ĀMEEN:

It is sunnah to say, Āmeen, when a person finishes recitation of Surah Fatihah. If he is praying alone he should say "Āmeen" in silence and if he is praying with congregation behind an Imam then he should say Āmeen fairly loudly when the Imam finishes saying the last verse of Surah Fatihah. When saying Āmeen the voice of the whole congregation should resound at the same time.

There are many hadiths which prove that saying Āmeen aloud is Sunnah of the Holy Prophet (ﷺ) and it was the regular practice of the companions. We will mention a few of these hadiths here.

a) Naeem al Mujammar said: "I prayed behind Abu Hurairah (R.A.). He recited Bismillāh hir-rahma nir-raheem, then he recited surah Fatihah, and when he reached walad dal-leen, he said, 'Āmeen' after it, and the people behind him said Āmeen....."

(Bukhari).

b) Abu Hurairah (R.A.) reported that the Messenger of Allah (ﷺ) said: "When the Imam says Ghayril Maghdūbi 'alayhim walad dal-leen, all of you should say, 'Āmeen', because the Angels say Āmeen and the Imam says Āmeen. And whosoever says Āmeen and his voice blends with that of the angels he would be forgiven his sins." (Ahmad, Abu Dawūd, Nisai).

c) Aisha (R.A.) reported that the Messenger of Allah (ﷺ) said: "Jews are more envious of Muslims in two things, (a) our greeting someone with Assalamu 'alaykum and (b) saying Āmeen (aloud) behind the Imam." (Ahmad, Ibn Majah).

d) Atā said: "I found 200 of the companions praying in the mosque of the Prophet (ﷺ) and when the Imam said 'walad dalleen', I heard the echo of their voices resound with Āmeen."

RECITATION AFTER SURAH FATIHAH

It is sunnah for a person who is praying that he should read a surah from the Qurān after Fatihah in the first two rakats of the fard prayer. He can recite one or more surahs. Here are a few short Surahs which you can recite.

a) **Surah Ikhlas**

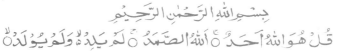

37

وَلَمْ يَكُنْ لَّهُ كُفُوًا اَحَدٌ

"*Qul huwal lāhu aḥad.*
Allāh huṣ-ṣamad.
Lam yalid walam yūlad.
Walam yakul-lahū Kufuwan aḥad."

"Say: He is Allah, the only one.
Allah helps and does not need help.
He does not produce a child, and He
Was not born of anyone.
There is no one equal to Him."

b) Surah Falaq.

بِسْمِ اللهِ الرَّحْمٰنِ الرَّحِيْمِ ۝
قُلْ اَعُوْذُ بِرَبِّ الْفَلَقِ ۝ مِنْ شَرِّ مَا خَلَقَ ۝ وَمِنْ شَرِّ
غَاسِقٍ اِذَا وَقَبَ ۝ وَمِنْ شَرِّ النَّفّاثَاتِ فِى الْعُقَدِ ۝ وَمِنْ
شَرِّ حَاسِدٍ اِذَا حَسَدَ ۝

"*Qul A'ūẓubi rab-bil falaq.*
Min shar-rimā Khalaq.
Wa min shar-ri ghāsiqin iẓa waqab.
Wa min shar-rin naf-fāthāti fil 'uqad.
Wa min shar-ri ḥāsidin i ẓā ḥasad."

"Say: I seek refuge in the Lord of the dawn,
from the evil of all that He has created,
and from the evil of the darkness of night when it falls,
and from the evil of those (charmers) who blow into knots.
And from the evil of the envier when he envies."

c) Surah Nas.

بِسْمِ اللهِ الرَّحْمٰنِ الرَّحِيْمِ ۞

قُلْ اَعُوْذُ بِرَبِّ النَّاسِ ۞ مَلِكِ النَّاسِ ۞ اِلٰهِ النَّاسِ ۞

مِنْ شَرِّ الْوَسْوَاسِ ۙ الْخَنَّاسِ ۞ اَلَّذِيْ يُوَسْوِسُ فِيْ صُدُوْرِ النَّاسِ ۞

مِنَ الْجِنَّةِ وَالنَّاسِ ۞

"Qul A'ūzubi rab-bin nās
Malikin nās. Ilā hin-nās.
Min shar-ril waswā sil khan-nās.
Allaẓi yuwaswisu fee ṣudū rin-nās.
Minal jin-nati wan-nās."

"Say: I seek refuge in the Sustainer of Mankind,
the Owner of Mankind, Lord of Mankind.
From the evil of the sneaking whisperer.
Who whispers in the hearts of mankind.
(Whether he be) from among jinns or mankind."

RUKU — BOWING

Then the person praying should say, "Allāhu Akbar", raising both
his hands to shoulder level with the palms facing outwards and fingers stretching to earlobes. He should then bend in ruku so that his
trunk (i.e. from head to hips) is perpendicular to the rest of the
body. His hands should rest on his knees with the fingers spread
apart, taking care that his arms do not touch his body. The person
should be calm and composed in the ruku position and not hurry it.
Then he should read: "Subḥāna rabbi yal aẓeem" at least three
times.

(۱) سُبْحَانَ رَبِّيَ الْعَظِيْمِ ۞

Subhāna Rabbi yāl Azim

This means:
"Glory be to my Lord who is the very greatest."
He can read it (3, 5, 7, 9, 11, etc.) times.
There are some other du'ās which can be read with subhāna rab-

39

bi yal azeem or instead of subhāna rab-bi yal azeem. Two of them are mentioned below:-

Other Du'ās in Ruku:
Aisha (R.A.) reported that the messenger of Allah (ﷺ) mostly read the following du'ā in his ruku and sajdah.

$$ \text{(٢) سُبْحَانَكَ اللّٰهُمَّ رَبَّنَا وَبِحَمْدِكَ اللّٰهُمَّ اغْفِرْلِيْ ه(بخارى،مسلم)} $$

"Subhāna Kallā humma rab-banā wabihamdika
Allāh hum maghfirlee."

This means:
"Glory be to you, oh our Lord, and all praise be to you. Oh Allah, forgive me." (Bukhari, Muslim).

Ali (R.A.) reported that the Messenger of Allah used to read the following Du'ā in Ruku:

$$ \text{(٣) اللّٰهُمَّ لَكَ رَكَعْتُ وَبِكَ اٰمَنْتُ وَلَكَ اَسْلَمْتُ اَنْتَ رَبِّيْ خَشِعَ سَمْعِيْ وَبَصَرِيْ وَمُخِّيْ وَعَظْمِيْ وَعَصَبِيْ0 وَمَا اسْتَقَلَّتْ بِهِ قَدَمَيَّ لِلّٰهِ رَبِّ الْعَالَمِيْنَ 0 (احمد،مسلم،ابوداؤد)} $$

"Allāh humma laka Raka'tu,
wabika āmantu,
walaka aslamtu,
anta rab-bī khashi'a sam'ee
Wabasaree wa mukh-khee wa'azmee
wa 'asabee wa masta qal - lat
bihee qada may-ya lil-lāhi.
rab-bil 'ālameen."

"O my Lord, I bowed to you and I believed in you and I submitted to you. You are my Lord. My ear, my sight, my brain, my bones, my tendons and whatever has been carried by my feet is submitted for the Lord of the worlds." (Ahmad, Muslim, Abu Dawūd, etc.)

40

There are other du'ās which Prophet Muhammad (ﷺ) read in Ruku and they can be found in other Books of Hadith.

Perfection of Ruku and Sajdah.

Abi Masud al Badri (R.A.) reported that the Messenger of Allah (ﷺ) said:

"Allah does not consider the prayer of a man who does not straighten his back when bowing for Ruku and performing Sajdah." (Ibn Khuzaimah, Ibn Hibban, Tabrani).

Abi Qatādah (R.A.) reported that the Messenger of Allah (ﷺ) said: "The worst thief is one who steals in his prayer."

Then the companions asked, "How can someone steal from his prayer?"

Prophet (ﷺ) answered, "He does not complete his Ruku and Sajdah with perfection." Or he said, "He does not make his back straight in Ruku and Sajdah." (Ahmad, Tabrani, Ibn Khuzaimah, Hakim).

These hadiths prove that Ruku and Sajdah should be done calmly, slowly and perfectly, otherwise salat of the person will be deficient.

QAWMAH (STANDING AFTER RUKU)

After the perfect Ruku the person praying should raise his head from Ruku saying:-

"Sami 'allāh hu liman ḥamidah"

"Verily Allah listens to one who praises Him." and *raise his hands up to the level of his shoulders with palms facing outwards and fingers stretched to the earlobes and then he should lower his hands to his sides. In the standing position he should be erect so that the joints of his body go back in place. While in this position he should recite one or all of the following du'ās as many times as he likes.

DU'ĀS IN QAWMAH

a) *"Rab-banā lakal ḥamad."* رَبَّنَا لَكَ الْحَمْدُ ٥

"O our Lord, all the praises be to you."

b) *"Rab-banā lakal ḥamd, ḥamdan Katheeran tayyiban mubarakan fee."*

رَبَّنَا لَكَ الْحَمْدُ حَمْدًا كَثِيْرًا طَيِّبًا مُبَارَكًا فِيْهِ ٥

"Oh our Lord, all praises be to you,
Very many, pure and blessed praises be to you."

c) Abi Sa'eed al Khudree (R.A.) says that when the Messenger of Allah (ﷺ) used to say:
"Sami 'allāh hu liman ḥamidah" he would follow it with:-

اَللّٰهُمَّ رَبَّنَا لَكَ الْحَمْدُ مِلْأُ السَّمَاوَاتِ وَمِلْأُ الْأَرْضِ وَمِلْأُ
مَا شِئْتَ مِنْ شَىْءٍ بَعْدُ اَهْلَ الثَّنَاءِ وَالْمَجْدِ اَحَقُّ مَا قَالَ
الْعَبْدُ وَكُلُّنَا لَكَ عَبْدٌ ـ اَللّٰهُمَّ لَا مَانِعَ لِمَا اَعْطَيْتَ وَلَا
مُعْطِىَ لِمَا مَنَعْتَ وَلَا يَنْفَعُ ذَا الْجَدِّ مِنْكَ الْجَدُّ ـ

(مسلم، احمد ابوداؤد)

FOOTNOTE --
*Some people get very annoyed when they see someone raising his hands while going into Ruku and again raising his hands while lifting his head from Ruku.

There are, however, authentic hadiths which prove that Prophet Muhammad (ﷺ) used to raise his hands at the beginning of prayer, before and after Ruku and when standing up for the third rakat. Every single Book of Hadith like Bukhari, Muslim, Muatta Imam Malik, Abu Dawūd, Tirmizi, Nisai, Ibn Majah, Ibn Khuzaimah, Hakim, Ahmad, Shafiee, Tabrani, Baihaqi, etc. etc. mentions these hadiths. Nearly four hundred companions also narrate this practice of Prophet Muhammad (ﷺ). So, there is not the slightest doubt that the raising of hands is sunnat and a person who practises this sunnat gets a greater reward than the person who does not practise it. However, even though the action is mentioned in the hadiths, all the ulamas agree that the prayer of a person who does not raise his hands is acceptable. Therefore, Muslims should not fight over this issue. If someone does not wish to raise his hands he should not discourage others from doing so because it is not a major controversial point.

"Allāh humma rab-banā lakal hamdu mil as
samāwāti wa mil al ardi wa mil amā
shiìa min shayin ba'du: ah lath-
thanāee wal majdi ahaq-qu mā qālal
'abdu Wa Kullu-na Laka'abd, Allāh humma
lā māni'a limā a'tayta walā mu'tiya limā
mana'ta walā yanfa'u zal jad-di minkal jad."

"O Allah, our Lord, all praises be to you, as much as they can fill
the heavens and earth and everything which you want to be filled
after that. You deserve to be praised and glorified. You deserve
more than what your servant has said and all of us are your slaves.
Nobody can prevent whatever you want to give and nobody can
give whatever you want to prevent and a person with high rank cannot benefit himself or another from his high rank against your
will."

(Muslim, Ahmad, Abu Dawūd).

There are some other du'ās which can be read in the Qawmah
position and these can be found in other Books of Hadith.

FIRST SAJDAH (PROSTRATION).

After the perfect qawmah the person praying should move to
perform sajdah saying:-

"Allāhu Akbar," putting palms downwards on the ground below
the ears. The knees should be brought downwards on the ground.
His fingers and toes should be pointing towards Qiblah without
spreading the fingers of the hands. During prostration seven parts
of the body should touch the ground:

(i)   the forehead along with the tip of the nose.
(ii)   both hands.
(iii)   both knees.
(iv)   the bottom surface of the toes of both feet.

In this position he should say:-   (١) سُبْحَانَ رَبِّيَ الْأَعْلَى

"Subḥāna Rabbi yal a'lā"

43

He should say this at least 3 times or 5, 7, 9, 11, etc. times.
"O Allah, glory be to you, the most high."
There are some other du'ās which can be read in the sajdah position.

OTHER DU'ĀS IN SAJDAH

1) Ali (R.A.) said that the Massenger of Allah (ﷺ)
    used to say while doing sajdah:-

(٢) اَللّٰهُمَّ لَكَ سَجَدْتُ وَبِكَ اٰمَنْتُ وَلَكَ اَسْلَمْتُ سَجَدَ
وَجْهِىَ لِلَّذِىْ خَلَقَهُ وَصَوَّرَهُ فَاَحْسَنَ صُوَرَهُ وَشَقَّ سَمْعَهُ
وَبَصَرَهُ فَتَبَارَكَ اللّٰهُ اَحْسَنُ الْخَالِقِيْنَ ۰ (مسلم)

"Allāh humma laka sajadtu, wabika āmantu,
walaka aslamtu,
sajada wajhiya lil-lazee Khalaqahū
Wasaw-warahū fa ahsana suwarahū,
Washaq-qa sam'ahū wabasarahū
fatabāra kal-lāhu ahsanul khāliqeen ."

"O Allah, for you I have prostrated, and in you I have faith, and unto you I have submitted, my forehead has prostrated in front of one who created it and gave shape to it and made it perfectly. Then he gave power of hearing and sight and blessed be Allah's name who is the Perfect Creator." (Muslim)

(ii) Abu Hurairah (R.A.) said that the Messenger of Allah
     (ﷺ) used to say in his sajdah:-

(٣) اَللّٰهُمَّ اغْفِرْلِىْ ذَنْبِىْ كُلَّهُ دِقَّهُ وَجِلَّهُ اَوَّلَهُ وَاٰخِرَهُ وَعَلَانِيَتَهُ
وَسِرَّهُ ـ (مُسْلِم)

Allāh hum maghfirlee żanbee kul-lahū diq-qahū ,
wa jil-lahū   aw-walahū wa ākhirahū, wa
'alā niy-yatahū wa sir-rahū."

44

"O Allah, forgive all my sins, minor
ones and major ones,
Ones I committed previously and
Ones I commit in the future.
Ones I commit openly
And ones I commit secretly."

(Muslim, Abu Dawūd, Hakim)

There are some other du'ās which the Messenger of Allah
(ﷺ) used to say in his Sajdah but these du'ās are too long to
mention here. They can be found in authentic Books of Hadith like
Muslim, Ahmad, Nisai Abu Dawūd, etc. It is not surprising that
Prophet Muhammad (ﷺ) stayed in Ruku and Sajdah for long
intervals.

All of the authentically approved du'ās can be said with   subhāna Rabbi yal a'lā or on their own or altogether according to the
time available and capacity of the person.

In the Sajdah position the worshipper is at his closest to Allah.
Hence, Sajdah should be performed calmly, and quietly, without
fidgeting, and the worshipper should try to read as many du'ās as he
possibly can.

JALSAH (SITTING BETWEEN TWO SAJDAH)

After performing one sajdah perfectly and calmly, the person
praying should raise his head from Sajdah saying, "Allāhu Akbar",
bending the left foot and sitting on it while keeping the right foot
propped up with its toes pointing towards the Qiblah, the palms of
his hands should rest on his thighs and knees. The back should be
straight so that the joints go back in place. It is sunnat to say the following du'ās while sitting in between the two sajdahs.

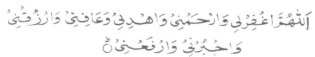

*"Allāh hum maghfirlee warhamnee wahdinee
wa 'āfinee warzuqnee wajburnee war fa'nee."*

45

"O Allah, forgive me, and have mercy on me,
and keep me on the right path,
and keep me healthy,
and provide me with halal sources of living,
and complete my shortcomings,
and make my rank high."

The worshipper can say this du'ā once or as many times as he likes.

SECOND SAJDAH

Then the person should perform the second sajdah, saying, "Allāhu Akbar" and repeat what he did in the first sajdah.

JALSAH-E-ISTARĀHAT (SITTING FOR REST)

Then he should raise his head up saying "Allāhu Akbar" and sit for a short while as he did in jalsah. He does this before standing up for the second rakat.

SECOND RAKAT

After standing up for the second rakat he should fold his hands over his chest as he did in the first rakat and start his recitation by reading "Bismilla.... ...and Surah Fatihah followed by any passage or a chapter of the Holy Quran." Then he should complete his second rakat in the manner of the first one.

While choosing a passage or a chapter for the recitation in the second or a subsequent rakat the worshipper should observe the order in which they occur in the Holy Qurān. Also, each Surah or verse should be shorter than the one recited before it. Hence, longer surahs are recited before shorter surahs.

TASHAHUD

After completing the last sajdah of the second rakat, the person should raise his head saying: "Allāhu Akbar". He should sit as he sat between the two sajdah, putting his left hand on his left knee and right hand on his right knee. The fist of the right hand is closed except for the index finger which is protruded. It is protruded so that the right thumb is brought to the second division of the index finger. In this position the person should read:-

اَلتَّحِيَّاتُ لِلّٰهِ وَالصَّلَوَاتُ وَالطَّيِّبَاتُ اَلسَّلَامُ عَلَيْكَ اَيُّهَا النَّبِيُّ وَرَحْمَةُ اللّٰهِ وَبَرَكَاتُهُ اَلسَّلَامُ عَلَيْنَا وَعَلٰى عِبَادِ اللّٰهِ الصَّالِحِينَ ٥ اَشْهَدُ اَنْ لَا اِلٰهَ اِلَّا اللّٰهُ وَاَشْهَدُ اَنَّ مُحَمَّدًا عَبْدُهُ وَرَسُولُهُ . (متفق عليه)

*"At-tahiy-yātu lil-lāhi was-salawātu wat-tay yibātu.
As-salāmu 'alayka ay-yuhan-nabiy-yu
wa rahma tullāhi wa barakātuhū
As-salāmu 'alaynā wa'alā 'ibādil-lā his-sāliheen."*

*"Ash hadu al lā ilāha illal lāhu
wa ash hadu an-na Muhammadan
'ab-duhū wa rasūluh."*

"All compliments, all physical prayer,
and all monitary worship are for Allah.
Peace be upon you, O Prophet,
and Allah's mercy and blessings.
Peace be on us and on all righteous
slaves of Allah."

(Bukhari and Muslim)

"I bear witness that no one is worthy of
worship except Allah.
And I bear witness that Muhammad
(ﷺ) is His slave and Messenger."

(Bukhari and Muslim)

47

While reading "Ash hadu — 'abduhū wa rasūluh." a person should raise the index finger of his right hand slightly and return it to its previous position after he has finished saying it.

A person praying 2 rakats only should continue to the next stage which is Salat Alan-Nabi (Darūd).

STANDING UP FOR THE THIRD RAKAT

If a person is praying three or four rakats, then he should stand up after tashahud saying "Allāhu Akbar" and raising his hands as he did in Takbeer Tahrimah start his recitation with "Bismillāh.....and then Surah Fatihah." In the third or fourth rakat of fard prayer recitation of Fatihah is sufficient. There is no need to say another Surah. But a person praying sunnat or nafl prayer can read a surah after Fatihah. After recitation he should continue to complete his third rakat (or fourth rakat if he is praying four).

After the completion of last rakat he should sit for tashahud as described above (as he sat after praying 2 rakats).

After Tashahud he should read Salat Alan-Nabi (Darūd; as follows:-

اَللّٰهُمَّ صَلِّ عَلٰى مُحَمَّدٍ وَّعَلٰى اٰلِ مُحَمَّدٍ كَمَا صَلَّيْتَ عَلٰى اِبْرَاهِيْمَ وَعَلٰى اٰلِ اِبْرَاهِيْمَ اِنَّكَ حَمِيْدٌ مَّجِيْدٌ ۔ اَللّٰهُمَّ بَارِكْ عَلٰى مُحَمَّدٍ وَّعَلٰى اٰلِ مُحَمَّدٍ كَمَا بَارَكْتَ عَلٰى اِبْرَاهِيْمَ وَعَلٰى اٰلِ اِبْرَاهِيْمَ اِنَّكَ حَمِيْدٌ مَّجِيْدٌ ۔

"Allāh humma ṣal-li 'alā Muḥammadin
wa 'alā āli Muḥammadin,
Kamā ṣal-layta 'alā Ibrāheema
Wa'alā āli Ibrāheema
innaka ḥameedum majeed."

"O Allah, send grace and honour on
Muhammad (ﷺ) and

on the family and true followers of Muhammad (ﷺ),
just as you sent Grace and Honour on
Ibrahim عليه السلام
and on the family and true followers of Ibrahim عليه السلام
Surely, you are praiseworthy, the Great."

"Allāh humma bārik 'alā Muhammadin
wa 'alā āli Muhammadin,
Kamā bārakta 'alā Ibrāheema
Wa'alā āli Ibrāheema
innaka hameedum majeed."

"O Allah, send your blessing on Muhammad (ﷺ)
and on the true followers of Muhammad (ﷺ), just
as you sent blessings on Ibrahim عليه السلام
and on his true followers.
Surely, you are praiseworthy, the Great."

DU'ĀS AFTER SALAT ALAN-NABI (DARŪD)

There are quite a lot of du'ās which Prophet (S.A.W.) used to
say after Darūd and he taught them to the companions. Here we
will mention a few of them.

i) Abdullah bin Amr (R.A.) said that Abu Bakr (R.A.) said to
the Messenger of Allah, "Please teach me a du'ā so I can say it
in my prayer."
So the Messenger of Allah (ﷺ) said,
"Say:-

(١) اَللّٰهُمَّ اِنِّیْ ظَلَمْتُ نَفْسِیْ ظُلْمًا کَثِیْرًا وَّلَا یَغْفِرُ الذُّنُوْبَ
اِلَّا اَنْتَ فَاغْفِرْلِیْ مَغْفِرَةً مِّنْ عِنْدِکَ وَارْحَمْنِیْ اِنَّکَ اَنْتَ
الْغَفُوْرُ الرَّحِیْمُ (بخاری و مسلم)

"Allāh humma innee zalamtu nafsee
Zulman, katheeran, walā yaghfi ruz zunuba
illā anta faghfirlee maghfiratam min
'indika, war hamnee innaka antal
ghafūrur raheem."

49

"O   Allah, I have been very cruel to myself (by ignoring my duty to you) and there is no one who can forgive the sins except you. So forgive me because you are the only forgiver and have mercy on me. Verily, you are the forgiver and merciful."

(Bukhari and Muslim)

ii) Shadād bin Aus (R.A.) reported that the Prophet of Allah (ﷺ) used to say in his prayer:-

(٢) اَللّٰهُمَّ اِنِّیْ اَسْئَلُكَ الثَّبَاتَ فِی الْاَمْرِ وَالْعَزِیْمَةَ عَلَی الرُّشْدِ
وَاَسْئَلُكَ شُكْرَ نِعْمَتِكَ وَحُسْنَ عِبَادَتِكَ وَاَسْئَلُكَ قَلْبًا
سَلِیْمًا وَّ لِسَانًا صَادِقًا وَاَسْئَلُكَ مِنْ خَیْرِ مَا تَعْـلَمُ
وَاَعُوْذُ بِكَ مِنْ شَرِّ مَا تَعْلَمُ وَاَسْتَغْفِرُكَ لِمَا تَعْلَمُ. (نسائی)

"Allāh humma innee as-alu kath thubāta
fil amri, wal 'azeemata 'alar rushdi,
wa as-aluka shukra ni'matika,
wa husna 'ibādatika, wa as-aluka
qalban saleeman, wa lisānan sādiqan,
wa as-aluka min khayri mā
Ta'lamu, wa aūžubika min
Shar-ri mā ta'lamu, wa as taghfiruka,
limā ta'lamu."

"O   Allah, I ask you for strength in every matter of deen and a strong willpower to be on the right path. And I ask you to make me thankful for your bounties and give me ability to worship you perfectly. And I ask you to make my heart sincere and my tongue truthful. I ask you for every goodness known to you and I seek refuge in you from everything bad that you know is bad. I ask your forgiveness for all mistakes you know." (Nisai).

(iii)   Aisha (R.A.) reported that the Prophet (ﷺ) used to
say this du'ā in his prayers:-

اَللّٰهُمَّ اِنِّى اَعُوْذُبِكَ مِنْ عَذَابِ الْقَبْرِ وَاَعُوْذُبِكَ مِنْ فِتْنَةِ
الدَّجَّالِ وَاَعُوْذُبِكَ مِنْ فِتْنَةِ الْمَحْيَا وَالْمَـمَاتِ ۔
اَللّٰهُمَّ اِنِّى اَعُوْذُبِكَ مِنَ الْمَأْثَمِ وَالْمَغْرَمِ (بخارى و مسلم)

"Allāh ḥumma innee A'ūzubika min
aẓābil qabri, wa A'ūzubika min
fitna tid daj-jāli, wa A'ūzubika
min fitna til maḥyā wal mamāt.
Allāh ḥumma innee A'ūzubika minal
mathami wal maghrami."

"O Allah I seek refuge in you from the punishment of the
grave, and I seek refuge in you from the troubles of daj-jal,
and I seek refuge in you from the difficulties and troubles
of the life and death. O Allah, I seek refuge in you from
every kind of sin and unexpected troubles."
(Bukhari and Muslim)

رَبِّ اجْعَلْنِىْ مُقِيْمَ الصَّلٰوةِ وَمِنْ ذُرِّيَّتِىْ رَبَّنَا وَتَقَبَّلْ
دُعَآءِ رَبَّنَا اغْفِرْلِىْ وَلِوَالِدَىَّ وَلِلْمُؤْمِنِيْنَ يَوْمَ يَقُوْمُ
الْحِسَابُ

(iv) *'Rab-bij 'alnee muqeemas salati wa min*
zur-riy yatee rab-banā wata qab-bal
du'ā, rab-ba naghfirlee waliwaliday-ya
wa lil mumineena yawma yaqūmul hisāb."

51

"O Lord, make me and my children keep up prayers,
Our Lord, accept our prayer,
Our Lord, forgive meand my parents
and all the Believers on the Day of Judgement."

Although most people read Rab bij'alnee after Darūd; it is per-
mitted to recite any nice du'ā. However, it should be known that
this du'ā is not one of those du'ās which Prophet (🕋) used to
say after Darūd. It is preferable to read both <u>Rab bij</u>'alnee and the
du'ās which are authentically proved from the Prophet (🕋)
and those he taught to his companions. We have mentioned only
four but there are about twelve. However, they are too lengthy to
mention here.

ENDING THE PRAYER

After praying for himself as much as the person wishes he should
end his prayer saying:-

"As-salāmu 'alaykum wa rahmatul lāh,"

"Peace be on you and the mercy of Allah,"
turning the face to the right and then to the left, both times over the
shoulder.
This brings the two, three or four rakats of the prayer to completion.

DU'ĀS AFTER SALUTATIONS

There are many du'ās which Prophet Muhammad (🕋)
used to say after salutation. So, a person praying should try to
memorise them and follow the practice of Prophet Muhammad
(🕋). Some of these du'ās we will mention here.

It was the continuous practice of Prophet Muhammad (🕋)
when he turned away from his prayer to say:-

1.

(١) اَللهُ أَكْبَرُ ن

(٢) أَسْتَغْفِرُاللهَ ن اَسْتَغْفِرُاللهَ ن اَسْتَغْفِرُاللهَ ن

(٣) اَللّٰهُمَّ اَنْتَ السَّلَامُ وَمِنْكَ السَّلَامُ تَبَارَكْتَ يَا ذَا الْجَلَالِ وَالْاِكْرَامِ ۵ (مُسْلِم)

a) Allāhu Akbar (once aloud)
   (Allah is the greatest)
b) Astagh firul-lāh (3 times)
   (I ask Allah to forgive me)
c) Allāh humma antas salāmu
   Wa minkas salāmu
   tabārakta yā Zaljalāli wal ikrām.

O Allah, you are the peace,
And you are the source of peace,
you are blessed, O possessor of Glory
and Honour. (MUSLIM)

اَللّٰهُمَّ اَعِنِّيْ عَلٰى ذِكْرِكَ وَشُكْرِكَ وَحُسْنِ عِبَادَتِكَ ۵

2. *"Allāh humma a'innee alā Żikrika
   wa shukrika wa hunsni 'ibādatika."*

"O Allah, help me to remember you all the time,
And to thank you, and to worship you perfectly."

(Ahmad, Abu Dawūd)

لَا اِلٰهَ اِلَّا اللهُ وَحْدَهُ وَحْدَهُ لَا شَرِيْكَ لَهُ ۵ وَلَهُ الْحَمْدُ وَهُوَ عَلٰى كُلِّ شَيْءٍ قَدِيْرٌ ۵ اَللّٰهُمَّ لَا مَانِعَ لِمَا اَعْطَيْتَ وَلَا مُعْطِيَ لِمَا مَنَعْتَ وَلَا يَنْفَعُ ذَا الْجَدِّ مِنْكَ الْجَدُّ ۵ (بخارى ومسلم)

3. a) *"Lā ilāha illal lāhū wahdahū lā shareeka lahū.
      Lahul Mulku wala hul hamdu
      wa huwa 'alā kul-li shay-in qadeer."*

53

b) "Allāh humma lā māni`a limā a`tayta
wa lā mu`tiya limā mana`ta wa lā
yanfa`u ż aljad-di minkal jad."

a) *"There is no God but Allah,*
He is the only one and has no partner,
Sovereignty and praise are only for Him.
and He has full authority over everything."

b) "Nobody can prevent whatever you want
to give and nobody can give whatever you
want to prevent and a person with high
rank cannot benefit himself or another
from his high rank against your will.

(Bukhari and Muslim)

سُبْحَانَ اللهِ 33 - اَلْحَمْدُ لِلّٰهِ 33 - اَللّٰهُ اَكْبَرُ 34

4. It is sunnat to say subhā nallāh (33 times), "Glory be to Allah."

Alhamdu lillāh (33 times), "Praise be to Allah."

and Allāhu Akbar (34 times), "Allah is the greatest."

There are very many du'ās which Prophet Muhammad (ﷺ)
used to say and he taught them to his companions. These can be
found in famous Books of Hadith.

Chapter 5

SAJDAH SAHEV
(SAJDAH FOR FORGETFULNESS)

If a person makes a mistake during his prayer what should he do?
Sajdah Sahev is allowed when a person praying becomes confused or forgets the number of rakats he has performed.

or

(ii)   He gets up after the second rakat when he should have remained in the sitting position and recited tashahud.
.2 sajdah before the salutation, then he said the salutation.

(Bukhari, Muslim)

In either of these cases the person has to base his prayer on the certainty of his memory and do 2 sajdah (Sajdah Sahev) before the salutation. In other words, Sajdah Sahev compensates the shortcoming in the prayer.

Abdullah bin Bujainah (R.A.) narrated that the Messenger of Allah (ﷺ) led them in the Zuhr prayer. He stood up after the first 2 raka.s and didn't sit for tashahud; so the people stood up with him as well. When he had completed the prayer and the people were waiting for his salutation: he said, 'Allahū Akbar' while he was sitting and did 2 sajdah before the salutation.Then he said the salutation.

(Bukhari, Muslim).

Abu Sa'eed al Khudri (R.A.) narrated that the Messenger of Allah (ﷺ) said,"When one of you becomes confused during his prayer and he doesn't know how many rakats he offered (3 or 4), he should ignore what is doubtful and base his prayer on what he believes is certain. Then he should do 2 extra sajdah before the salutation. If he had prayed five rakats, then these 2 sajdah will make his prayer 6 rakats (2 of which will be nafl), and if he had prayed the correct number of rakats then these 2 sajdah will be humility for the devil." (Muslim).

55

These ahadith prove that Sajdah Sahev should be done before the salutation but there are hadiths which prove that the Prophet (ﷺ) did 2 sajdah (Sajdah Sahev) after the salutation.

Abdullah bin Ja'far (R.A.) narrated from the Prophet (ﷺ) that he said, "Anyone who has become confused and doubtful in his prayer he should do 2 extra sajdah after he has given the salutation."

(Ahmad, Abu Dawūd, Nisai, Ibn Khuzaimah).

There is no contradiction between these hadiths. Both ways are proved by the Prophet (ﷺ). It is up to the believer to choose one. They can both be practised but it seems that the first method, that is, doing 2 sajdah just before the salutation, is more reasonable, more authentic and more widely practised by the Muhadditheen and ulama.

WHEN CAN A PERSON DO SAJDAH SAHEV

1. If somebody is doubtful about the number of rakats he prayed.
2. If he forgets to sit in the first tashahud and gets up for the third rakat.
3. If he finishes his prayer forgetfully without completing the number of rakats he intended to pray.

Note: Sajdah Sahev could not be a sufficient replacement for missing the actions of the prayer which are considered as rukun of the prayer; for example, Qiyam (standing position between Takbeer Tahrima and ruku), ruku, and sajdah.

PRAYING IN CONGREGATION

When praying fard in congregation the Imam has to recite surah Fatihah and any chapter or part of the Quran aloud, in the Fajr prayer, first 2 rakats of the maghrib prayer and the first 2 rakats of the Isha prayer. It means the Imam will recite in silence in the Zuhr and Asr prayer.

Congregational prayer is almost obligatory in Fard prayer but there are some occasional optional prayers which are preferable to offer in congregation; for example, Eid prayer, Taraweeh prayer, Rain prayer, etc.). However, it is preferable to pray the usual nafl prayer alone.

Every prayer must be started with Takbeer Tahrima and finished with a salutation.

Chapter 6

OCCASIONAL PRAYERS

WITR PRAYER

Witr Prayer is sunnat Mu'akkadah. It is very much emphasized by Prophet Muhammad (鐌). He did not leave this prayer even during a journey or when mounted on camelback.

It was so much emphasized that some Muslim scholars understood that it was wajib (compulsory) but after a careful study of hadiths it can be said that it is not wajib but a very much emphasized prayer.

Witr prayer is often mistakenly thought of as part of the Isha prayer. This is not so. Witr prayer is a separate prayer which can be offered after the Isha prayer right up to the break of dawn. For the convenience of the believers the Prophet (鐌) allowed Witrs to be offered straight after Isha.

In Arabic the word witr means, One. In hadiths the Messenger of Allah (鐌) said: "Allah is one, so he likes the number, ONE."

(Muslim)

Allah also likes odd numbers because when an odd number is divided by 2, the remainder is always one. For this reason Prophet (鐌) preferred odd numbers. He liked to do things in odd numbers in his routine life, also, such as: when saying prayers, saying du'ās, eating dates, etc. That is why Prophet (鐌) asked the believers to pray witr at the end of the night prayer so that it can make the night prayer into an odd number.

Abdullah bin Umar (R.A.) says that the Messenger of Allah (鐌) said: "Night prayer is to be offered in 2 rakats units. When one of you feels that dawn is near then he should offer 1 rakat which can make all the night prayer he offered into an odd number."

(Bukhari, Muslim)

NUMBER OF RAKATS OF WITR PRAYER

Abdullah bin Umar (R.A.) said that the Messenger of Allah (ﷺ) said: "Witr prayer is one rakat at the end of the nafl prayer at night."

Abu Ayub (R.A.) said that the Prophet Muhammad (ﷺ) said: "Every Muslim should pray witr. Anyone who likes to pray 5 rakats of witr he should do so, anyone who likes to pray 3 rakats, he should do so, and anyone who likes to pray one rakat, he should do so."

(Abu Dawūd, Nisai, Ibn Majah).

We understand from the above mentioned hadiths that the actual witr prayer is one rakat, although a person can offer, 1, 3, 5, 7, or 9 rakats of witr prayer. All of these numbers are approved by Prophet Muhammad (ﷺ) in authentic hadiths.

TIME OF WITR PRAYER

Witr prayer can be offered after the Isha prayer right up to the break of dawn.

Aisha (R.A.) said: "Prophet Muhammad (ﷺ) prayed witr during all times of the night. Sometimes he prayed Witr during the first part of the night, sometimes during the middle part of the night, and sometimes during the end part of the night but he used to complete the prayer before the break of dawn."

(Bukhari, Muslim).

However, a person who thinks he could not get up to pray witr at the end part of the night can offer witr immediately after Isha or before he goes to bed. But someone who thinks that he can get up and pray nafl in the night should pray witr at the end of his night prayer.

Jabir (R.A.) said that the Prophet (ﷺ) said: "Anyone of you who could not get up at the end part of the night he should pray witr in the first part of the night and anyone of you who thinks he can get up at the end part of the night he should pray witr then, because the angels are present for the prayer offered at the end part of the night."

(Muslim, Ahmad, Tirmizi, Ibn Majah).

59

HOW TO PRAY WITR

When praying one Witr a person can offer it as the usual prayer.

When praying 3, 5, 7 or 9 rakats of witr prayer there is more than one way the prayer can be offered.

For example:-

a) A person praying 3 rakats witr can pray 2 rakats like the usual prayer. After the Salutation, As-salāmu 'alaykum wa rahmatul-lāh, first to the right and then to the left he should get up immediately to complete the third rakat. This way of offering witr prayer is called, witr bil fasal'.

b) A person praying 3 rakats or 5 rakats Witr should not sit for Tashahud in between the rakats except in the last rakat.

c) A person praying 3, 5, or 7 rakats Witr should sit in Tashahud in the last but one rakat, e.g. in the second rakat if he is offering 3 Witr, fourth rakat if he is offering 5 witr, or sixth rakat if he is offering 7 Witr and so on. He should read Tashahud and then get up for the last rakat and complete it.

All 3 methods are authentic and are practised by the great ulamas and scholars. So Muslims can choose any one of these 3 methods to offer the witr prayer. When praying 3 rakats, witr, however, it is preferable to chose method 'a' or 'b' as Prophet Muhammad (ﷺ) said: "Do not make your witr prayer similar to your maghrib prayer."

(Qiamul-lail).

DU'Ā QUNŪT IN WITR PRAYER

Reading du'ā Qunūt in the last rakat of the Witr Prayer is proven from Prophet Muhammad (ﷺ) and it can be read before ruku or after ruku.

Humaid (R.A.) narrated, that he asked Anas (R.A.) about the du'ā Qunūt, whether it should be read before the ruku or after the ruku.

Anas (R.A.) replied, "We used to say it before the ruku and after the ruku."
(Ibn Majah, Qiamul-Lail of Muhammad bin Nasar al Marwazi, Fathul Bari).

Although du'ā Qunūt can be said before the ruku, it is more authentic and more approved to say it after the ruku.

a) Someone who wants to read Qunūt before ruku he should read it after he has finished reciting surah Fatihah and chapter of the Holy Quran. While reciting du'ā Qunūt a person can cup his hands in front of him or he can leave them folded.

b) Someone who wants to read Qunūt after the ruku he can read it with his hands cupped in front of him or he can let his hands rest at his sides. Saying du'ā after the ruku and cupping   hands in front   is preferable as this was the practice of Prophet Muhammad (ﷺ .).

Note: Some Fuqhas insist that reading du'ā Qunūt is compulsory in the last rakat of the Fajr prayer, but if you study hadiths carefully you will find that it is not compulsory either in the Witr or in the Fajr prayer. Therefore, if a person leaves du'ā Qunūt in his witr prayer his prayer will not be deficient. Also, if someone does not know du'ā Qunūt he need not say another chapter of the Quran or any other words in its replacement. Du'ā Qunūt can be read in any prayer.

TEXT OF DU'Ā QUNŪT

Hasan bin Ali (R.A.) said   "The Messenger of Allah (ﷺ) taught me the words which I should say in the du'ā of witr, and those are as follows:-

الّلهُمَّ اهْدِنِيْ فِيْمَنْ هَدَيْتَ وَعَافِنِيْ فِيْمَنْ عَافَيْتَ وَتَوَلَّنِيْ
فِيْمَنْ تَوَلَّيْتَ وَبَارِكْ لِيْ فِيْمَا اَعْطَيْتَ وَقِنِيْ شَرَّمَا قَضَيْتَ
فَاِنَّكَ تَقْضِيْ وَلاَ يُقْضَى عَلَيْكَ اِنَّهُ لاَيَذِلُّ مَنْ وَالَيْتَ
وَلاَ يَعِزُّ مَنْ عَادَيْتَ تَبَارَكْتَ رَبَّنَا وَتَعَالَيْتَ نَسْتَغْفِرُكَ
وَنَتُوْبُ اِلَيْكَ وَصَلَّى اللهُ عَلَى النَّبِيِّ

"Allāh hum mahdinee feeman hadayt,
Wa 'āfinee feeman 'āfayt,
wata wal-lanee feeman tawal-layt,
wa bārik lee feemā a'tait,
waqinee shar-ra mā qadayt,
fa-innaka taqdee walā yuqdā 'alayk,
innahū lā Yażil-lu manw wālayt,
walā ya'iz-zu man 'ādayt,
tabārakta rabbanā wata 'ālayt,
nastaghfiruka wanatubu ilayk,
Wa sal-lal lāhū alan-nabee."

"O Allah, make me among those whom you have guided, and
make me among those whom you have saved, and make me
among those whom you have chosen, and bless whatever you
have given me, and protect me from the evil which you have
decreed; verily, you decide the things and nobody can decide
against you; surely the· person you befriend   can't be dis-
graced, and the person you oppose   can't be honoured. You are
blessed, our Lord, and exalted, we ask for your forgiveness and
turn to you. Peace and mercy of Allah be upon the Prophet."

(Abu Dawūd, Nisai, Ibn Majah, Tirmizi).

b) اَللّهُمَّ اِنَّا نَسْتَعِيْنُكَ وَنَسْتَغْفِرُكَ وَنُؤْمِنُ بِكَ وَنَتَوَكَّلُ
عَلَيْكَ وَنُثْنِىْ عَلَيْكَ الْخَيْرَ وَنَشْكُرُكَ وَلاَ نَكْفُرُكَ وَنَخْلَعُ
وَنَتْرُكُ مَنْ يَفْجُرُكَ ـ اَللّهُمَّ اِيَّاكَ نَعْبُدُ وَلَكَ نُصَلِّىْ
وَنَسْجُدُ وَاِلَيْكَ نَسْعَى وَنَحْفِدُ وَنَرْجُوْ رَحْمَتَكَ وَنَخْشَى

62

$$\text{عَذَابَكَ اِنَّ عَذَابَكَ بِالْكُفَّارِ مُلْحِقٌ}$$

"Allāh humma in-nā nasta'eenuka wa nastaghfiruka wa mu'minubika wa natawak-kalu 'alayka wa nuthnee 'alayk-al khayr. Wa nashkuruka walā nakfuruka wa nakhla'u wa natruku man-y yafjurka. Allāh humma iyyāka na'budu walaka nusal-lee wa nas-judu wa ilayka nas'ā wa nahfidu wa narjū rahmataka wa nakhshā 'azābaka inna 'azābaka bil kuf-fāri mulhiq."

"O Allah, we ask you for help and seek your forgiveness, and we believe in you and have trust in you, and we praise you in the best way and we thank you and we are not ungrateful to you, and we forsake and turn away from the one who disobeys you. O Allah, we worship you only and pray to you and prostrate our-selves before you, and we run towards you and serve you, and we hope to receive your mercy, and we fear your punishment. Surely, the disbelievers will receive your punishment."

Some ulamas recommend this du'ā in the witr prayer. Of course, it can be read as it is a nice du'ā but it is not one of those du'ās which Prophet Muhammad (ﷺ) read in his Qunūt.

There are some other du'ās which Prophet Muhammad (ﷺ) used to read in his Qunūt in the Witr prayer or in his other prayers.

A person can read all these du'ās together or just one of them or combine them with other du'ās.

JUMAH (FRIDAY PRAYER)

IMPORTANCE OF ATTENDING FRIDAY PRAYER

Friday Prayer is very important in Islam. It has got its own moral, social and political benefits. It is obligatory for every Muslim except women, children, slaves, seriously ill people and travellers. They can pray Jumah but it is not obligatory on them.

Prophet Muhammad (ﷺ) has given a strong warning to a person who leaves his Jumah prayer without a good reason.

63

In one hadith Abdullah bin Masūd (R.A.) narrated what the Messenger of Allah (ﷺ) once said about the people who did not come to the Friday Prayer without a good reason.

"I wish to appoint someone to lead the prayer and myself go to the houses of those who missed the Friday Prayer and set fire to their houses with the occupants in them."

(Muslim, Ahmad).

Another hadith states, "A person who leaves 3 Friday prayers consecutively, Allah puts a seal on his heart."

(Ahmad, Tirmizi, abu Dawūd).

IMPORTANCE OF CLEANLINESS FOR FRIDAY PRAYER

Because in Friday Prayer a comparatively large number of Muslims gather in a big place, so, Islam emphasizes on the physical cleanliness as well.

Prophet (ﷺ) said, "A perosn who has a bath on Friday, cleanses himself fully, uses oil and perfume; then goes to the mosque early in the afternoon and takes his place quietly without pushing or disturbing people; then he prays (optional prayer as much as he was able to pray); then sits quietly listening to the Khutbah, he will be forgiven his sins between this Jumah and the next Jumah."

(Bukhari).

IMPORTANCE OF GOING EARLY TO FRIDAY PRAYER

On Friday it is more rewarding to get ready quickly to go to the mosque.

Abu Hurairah (R.A.) narrated that the Messenger of Allah (ﷺ) said, "On Friday the Angels stand at the door of the mosque and write down the names of the people in the order in which they enter the mosque for Friday prayer. The first group of people who enter the mosque get the reward equivalent to that of sacrificing a camel, the people who enter the mosque after them get the reward equivalent to that of sacrificing a cow. The people who enter the mosque after them get the reward equivalent to that of sacrificing a ram and the people who follow on likewise get the reward of a chicken, egg and so on there is a gradation of rewards for the people as they enter. The angels keep writing the names of the people as they enter the mosque until the Imam sits down to give Khutbah. Then the angels collect their registers and sit and listen to the Khutbah."

(Bukhari, Muslim).

PRAYER BEFORE JUMAH

A person who goes to attend Friday prayer can pray as many nafls as he wishes after the sun has declined from its zenith to when the Imam comes to give Khutbah. Anyhow he is expected to pray at least 2 rakats sunnat.

LISTENING TO KHUTBAH (SERMON)

Once the Khutbah starts, the whole congregation should listen to it in silence. If a person arrives while the Imam is giving Khutbah then this person should pray 2 rakats nafl before sitting down to listen to Khutbah.

Jabir (R.A.) said that the Messenger of Allah (ﷺ) said while he was giving Khutbah:

"If anyone of you goes to attend Friday Prayer while the Imam is delivering Khutbah he should pray 2 rakats and should not make them long."

(Muslim).

There is another hadith. Jabir (R.A.) says that once a man came to Friday Prayer while the Messenger of Allah (ﷺ) was delivering Khutbah, so Allah's messenger (ﷺ) asked him, "Did you pray?"

"No", he answered.

Then Prophet (ﷺ) said to him, "Stand up and pray".

(Bukhari, Muslim, Abu Dawūd, Tirmizi).

It is a continuous practice in some mosques that those who arrive while the Imam is giving speech sit down and listen to the speech. When the Imam has finished the speech he gives time to the late arrivals to pray 2 or 4 rakats sunnat. After that the Imam gives a short Khutbah in Arabic before praying the Jumah Prayer.

These people get very annoyed if they see a person offer 2 rakats sunnat while the Imam is giving speech. They feel that the person is being disrespectful to the Imam. This is incorrect and unproved from the practice of Prophet Muhammad (ﷺ)

It is also against those hadiths which we mentioned above and the one we are mentioning below.

Abi Qatadah (R.A.) says that the Messenger of Allah (ﷺ) said, "Whenever one of you enters the mosque he should not sit down without offering 2 rakats."

(Bukhari, Muslim).

These hadiths clarify the points which are mispractised above. The Imams and ulamas who have even a slight fear of Allah and respect for hadith and the sunnah of Prophet Muhammad (ﷺ) should stop this practice and should not become annoyed when others pray 2 rakats.

ACTUAL JUMAH PRAYER

Jumah Prayer is 2 rakats fard. If a person is late and finds only 1 rakat with the congregation he should complete the second rakat alone. If a person arrives so late that he misses the Jumah prayer completely then he has to offer 4 rakat fard of Zuhr prayer. The Jumah prayer is a replacement of Zuhr prayer but the Imam has to recite Qirāt aloud in Jumah Prayer.

PRAYER AFTER JUMAH

After the Jumah Prayer 2 rakats of sunnat prayer is an authentically proved practice of Prophet Muhammad (ﷺ) but some companions used to pray 4 or 6 rakats sunnat after the Jumah Prayer.

Ibn Umar (R.A.) said that the Messenger of Allah (ﷺ) did not pray after the Friday prayer until he went home and then he prayed 2 rakats.

(Bukhari, Muslim).

Abu Hurairah (R.A.) narrated that the Messenger of Allah (ﷺ) said: "Anyone of you who is going to pray after the Friday prayer, he should pray 4 rakats.

(Muslim).

Atā said: "Whenever Abdullah ibn Umar (R.A.) prayed Jumah in Makkah, he would move a little forward after the Jumah prayer and offer 2 rakats; then he would move a little forward again and offer 4 rakats. And whenever he prayed Jumah in Madinah, he did not pray in the mosque after the Jumah prayer until he got back home; then he prayed 2 rakats. When he was asked why he did not pray in the mosque after the Jumah prayer. He answered, 'This was the practice of Prophet Muhammad (ﷺ).'"

These hadiths clarify that 2, 4 or 6 rakats can be offered after the Jumah prayer according to the time and capacity of the person. It is not good practice to accuse people who read 2 rakats only because this, too, was the authentic practice of Prophet Muhammad (ﷺ).

EID PRAYER

Place for Eid Prayer

Eid prayer should be offered outdoor in the open, e.g. in a park field, or a desert, etc. If it is wet or not possible to find a suitable outdoor place it can be prayed in a mosque or a large hall.

(Abu Dawūd)

Time of Eid Prayer

Eid prayer should be offered when the sun can be seen clearly above the horizon.

Number of Rakats of Eid Prayer

Eid prayer is 2 rakats. There is no nafl prayer before or after the Eid Prayer. There is no Iqamat or azan for Eid Prayer.

Ibn Abbas (R.A.) reported: "No doubt, Prophet Muhammad (ﷺ) used to pray 2 rakats only for Eid Prayer. He did not pray anything before or afterwards."

(Bukhari, Muslim).

CONDUCT OF EID PRAYER

2 rakats of Eid prayer should be offered in the same manner as the 2 rakats of the usual prayer except that there are 7 Takbeers in the first rakat and five Takbeers in the second rakat. With each extra Takbeer the hands should be raised up to the shoulder level (as in Takbeer Tahrima).

All extra Takbeers should be pronounced before starting Qirāt (recitation).

Kathir bin Abdullah reported from his father and his father from grandfather that Prophet (ﷺ) said 7 Takbeers in the first rakat of Eid prayer and 5 Takbeers in the second rakat of Eid Prayer before beginning recitation.

(Tirmizi, Ibn Majah, Darmi).

EID PRAYER IS OFFERED BEFORE KHUTBAH

Jafar bin Muhammad (R.A.) reported:- "No doubt, Prophet Muhammad (ﷺ), Abu Bakr (R.A.),and Umar (R.A.) said 7 extra Takbeers in the first rakat of their Eid and Rain Prayer and five extra takbeers in the second rakat of their Eid and Rain Prayer. Prophet (ﷺ) offered Eid Prayer before Khutbah and recited aloud."

(Shafíee).

RAIN PRAYER

The Rain Prayer is a special prayer which is offered during a period of drought. Muslims are asked to pray 2 rakat nafl out in the open and make special du'ās especially for the rain.

JANAZAH PRAYER (FUNERAL PRAYER)

Janazah Prayer

It is a right of a Muslim that when he passes away other Muslims should pray Janazah prayer for him. Janazah prayer is supererogatory prayer. If no one from the whole of the Muslim Community prayed the Janazah prayer; then the whole community would be considered sinful in the sight of Allah. If some of the people prayed the Janazah prayer then the whole community is saved from the anger of Allah even though the reward will only be given to the participants only.

In hadiths Prophet Muhammad (ﷺ) emphasized and encouraged the Muslims to attend funeral ceremonies.. So, every Muslim male should try his best to fulfil his duty for the deceased.

1. Janazah prayer should be prayed in congregation as this is more rewardful. It can be prayed in more than one congregation but by different people.
2. Janazah prayer should be offered in an open place but in case of rain or bad weather or any other reason it can be prayed in a mosque or a hall, etc.

3. While Praying Janazah Prayer

The Imam should stand level with the head and shoulders of the dead body if the body is male. Imam should stand level with the middle part of the body if it is female.

4. Where Janazah Prayer Differs

Janazah prayer is only slightly different from other prayers in that there is no ruku, no sajdah, and no Tashahud in it. There is no fixed time for offering this prayer. It has to be prayed in a standing position only. Other conditions like purification, facing Qiblah, sutra, dress, etc. have to be satisfied as in the usual prayers.

5. Conduct of Janazah Prayer

a. Like other prayers facing Qiblah is a necessary condition. The Imam should ask the people to straighten their rows. There should be an odd number of rows as it is more rewardful.
b. Making intention is necessary in Janazah prayer as it is necessary in other prayers. Before beginning prayer the intention should be made in the heart as uttering any words of niyat aloud was not the practice of Prophet Muhammad (ﷺ) or of his companions.

c. **First Takbeer of Takbeer Tahrima**

Janazah prayer contains 4 Takbeers. First Takbeer is Takbeer Tahrima. The Imam says Allāhu Akbar and raises his hands up to the shoulder level with fingers stretching to the earlobes and the congregation does the same. Then the Imam folds his hands on his chest right hand over the left.

d. **Duā of Starting**

Duā of Starting. Then the person can read one of those du'ās which are recommended in the first rakat of the usual prayer before recitation of Fatihah. For example:

سُبْحَانَكَ اللّٰهُمَّ وَبِحَمْدِكَ وَتَبَارَكَ اسْمُكَ وَتَعَالٰى جَدُّكَ وَلَا اِلٰهَ غَيْرُكَ ط

"*Subhāna Kallā humma wabi hamdika wa tabāra kasmuka wata 'alā jad-duka walā ilāha ghayruk.*"

"Glory be to you, O Allah, and all praises are due unto you, and blessed is your name and high is your majesty and none is worthy of worship but you."

Or he can say other du'ās. Some scholars do not recommend du'ā of starting in Janazah prayer but reading it is preferable. However, if someone does not read it, it does not affect his prayer. Both ways are practised by Muslim scholars.

e. Then the person should say:-

اَعُوْذُ بِاللهِ مِنَ الشَّيْطَانِ الرَّجِيْمِ

بِسْمِ اللهِ الرَّحْمٰنِ الرَّحِيْمِ

"*A'ūzu bil-lāhi minash shaytā nir rajeem.*"

"*Bismillā hir-rahmā nir-raheem.*"

and then he should recite surah Fatihah.

اَلْحَمْدُ لِلّٰهِ رَبِّ الْعَالَمِيْنَ ۙ الرَّحْمٰنِ الرَّحِيْمِ ۙ مَالِكِ يَوْمِ الدِّيْنِ ۙ اِيَّاكَ نَعْبُدُ وَاِيَّاكَ نَسْتَعِيْنُ ۙ اِهْدِنَا الصِّرَاطَ الْمُسْتَقِيْمَ ۙ صِرَاطَ الَّذِيْنَ اَنْعَمْتَ عَلَيْهِمْ ۙ غَيْرِ الْمَغْضُوْبِ عَلَيْهِمْ وَلَا الضَّآلِّيْنَ ۙ

اٰمِيْن ۔

"Alhamdu lil-lāhi rab-bil 'ālameen.
Ar-rahmā nir-raheem.
Māliki yawmid - deen.
Iyyāka na'budu wa
iyyāka nasta'een.
Ihdinas sirātal mustaqeem.
Sirātal lazeena an'amta 'alayhim.
Ghayril maghdūbi
'alayhim walad dāl-leen. Āmeen."

"Praise is only for Allah, Lord
of the Universe.
The most kind, the most merciful.
The master of the Day of Judgement.
You alone we worship and to you alone
we pray for help.
Show us the straight way,
the way of those whom you have blessed.
Who have not deserved your anger,
Nor gone astray."

Some people do not read surah Fatihah in Janazah prayer but surah Fatihah is necessary for the validity of any type of prayer as Prophet Muhammad (ﷺ) has said that no prayer is valid without Fatihah.

Talhah bin Abdullah bin Aouf (R.A.) said that he prayed the Janazah prayer behind Abdullah bin Abbas (R.A.) and Abdullah bin Abbas (R.A.) read surah Fatihah aloud. Afterwards he said:

"I did read it out loud so that you may know that it is the sunnah of Prophet Muhammad (ﷺ)."

(Bukhari).

This hadith proves that reciting surah Fatihah is necessary in Janazah prayer as well.

6. RECITATION OF A SURAH

A chapter or part of a chapter can be read after the recitation of surah Fatihah but it is not essential to read it.

71

7. SECOND TAKBEER

Then the Imam should say the second takbeer and the congregation should follow but it is not necessary to raise the hands up to the shoulder level but if someone does, it is alright. Both ways are practised by great ulamas and scholars.

8. AFTER THE SECOND TAKBEER

After the second Takbeer the person praying Janazah should recite darūd in his heart. It is preferable to read the darūd which a person reads in Tashahud of his usual prayer.

9. THIRD TAKBEER

Then the Imam should say the third takbeer and the congregation should follow. Now, each person should pray for the deceased.

Alternatively the Imam can pray out loud and the congregation can say, Āmin, after him. All kinds of du'ās for the benefit of the deceased can be said. Some of these are mentioned below.

10. DU'Ā OF JANAZAH

a. Abu Hurairah (R.A.) said that the Messenger of Allah (ﷺ) prayed Janazah of a Muslim and he said in his du'ā (the following words):-

اَللّٰهُمَّ اغْفِرْ لِحَيِّنَا وَمَيِّتِنَا وَشَاهِدِنَا وَغَائِبِنَا وَصَغِيْرِنَا
وَكَبِيْرِنَا وَذَكَرِنَا وَأُنْثَانَا ـ اَللّٰهُمَّ مَنْ اَحْيَيْتَهُ مِنَّا
فَاَحْيِهِ عَلَى الْاِسْلَامِ وَمَنْ تَوَفَّيْتَهُ مِنَّا فَتَوَفَّهُ عَلَى
الْاِيْمَانِ اَللّٰهُمَّ لَا تَحْرِمْنَا اَجْرَهُ وَلَا تَفْتِنَّا بَعْدَهُ ـ مسلم

"Allāh hum maghfirli hay-yinā wa may-yitinā. wa shāhidinā wa ghā-ibinā, wa saghee rinā` wa kabeerinā wa zakarinā wa unthānā, Allāh humma man ahyaytahū min-nā fa ahyihee 'alal islām, waman tawaf-faytahu min-nā fatawaf-fahū 'alal īman. Allāh humma lā tahrimnā ajrahū walā taftin-nā ba'dahū."

72

"O Allah, forgive our people who are still alive and who have passed away, forgive those who are present here and those who are absent, forgive our young and our elderly, forgive our males and females. O Allah, the one whom you wish to keep alive from among us make him live according to Islam, and anyone whom you wish to die from among us, let him die in belief and faith. O Allah, do not deprive us from his reward and do not put us in fitna (hardship or any type of trial) after his death."

(Ahmad, Abu Dawūd, Tirmizi, Ibn Majah).

b. Aouf bin Malik (R.A.) said that the Messenger of Allah (ﷺ) prayed a Janazah prayer and I heard him saying the following du'ā and I memorised it.

اَللّٰهُمَّ اغْفِرْلَهُ وَارْحَمْهُ وَاعْفُ عَنْهُ وَعَافِهِ وَاَكْرِمْ نُزُلَهُ وَوَسِّعْ مُدْخَلَهُ وَاغْسِلْهُ بِالْمَاءِ وَالثَّلْجِ وَالْبَرْدِ وَنَقِّهِ مِنَ الْخَطَايَا كَمَا يُنَقَّى الثَّوْبُ الْاَبْيَضُ مِنَ الدَّنَسِ وَاَبْدِلْهُ دَارًا خَيْرًا مِنْ دَارِهِ وَاَهْلًا خَيْرًا مِنْ اَهْلِهِ وَزَوْجًا خَيْرًا مِنْ زَوْجِهِ وَاَدْخِلْهُ الْجَنَّةَ وَقِهِ فِتْنَةَ الْقَبْرِ وَعَذَابَ النَّارِ ، رَسُلَمْ،

"Allāh hum maghfirlahū warhamhū wa'fu 'anhu wa 'āfihee wa akrim nuzulahū wa was-si' mudkhalahū, waghsilhu bil māee wath thalji wal bardi, wa naq-qihī minal Khatāyā Kamā yunaq-qath thawbul abyadu minad danasi, wa abdilhu dāran Khayram min darihī, wa ahlan Khayram min ahlihī wa zawjan Khayram min zaw-jihī, wa adkhil hul jan-nata, waqihī fitnatal qabri wa 'azā ban nār."

"O Allah, forgive him, have mercy on him, pardon him, grant him security, provide him a nice place and spacious lodgings, wash him (of his sins) with water, snow and ice, purify him from his sins as a white garment is cleansed from dirt, replace his present abode with a better one, replace his present family with a better one, replace his present partner with a better one, make him enter paradise and save him from the trials of grave and the punishment of hell."

(Muslim).

73

c. Abu Hurairah (R.A.) said that the messenger of Allah (ﷺ) prayed and said:

اَللّٰهُمَّ اَنْتَ رَبُّهَا وَ اَنْتَ خَلَقْتَهَا وَ اَنْتَ رَزَقْتَهَا وَ اَنْتَ
هَدَيْتَهَا لِلْوِسْلَامِ وَ اَنْتَ قَبَضْتَ رُوْحَهَا وَ اَنْتَ اَعْلَمُ
بِسِرِّهَا وَ عَلَا نِيَّتِهَا جِئْنَا شُفَعَاءَ فَاغْفِرْلَهُ ذَنْبَهُ

(ابوداؤد ـ احمد)

"Allāh humma anta rab-buhā, wa anta Khalaqtahā, wa anta razaqtahā, wa anta hadaytahā lil islām, wa anta qabadta rūhahā, wa anta a'lamu bisir-rihā wa 'alā niy-yatihā, ji nā shufa'āà, faghfirlahū żanbahū".

"O Allah, you are its Lord, you have created it, and you have guided it towards Islam, and you have taken out his soul and you know best about its secret and open deeds. We have come as intercessors, so forgive him."

(Abu Dawūd, Ahamd).

One thing we can see clearly from the above mentioned hadiths that every companion who narrated the du'ā of Janazah prayer says that he heard the Prophet (ﷺ) saying the words of du'ā in Janazah prayer. This proves that the Messenger of Allah (ﷺ) used to say the Janazah prayer or at least the du'ās in Janazah prayer aloud. Therefore, there should not be any objection or confusion if the Imam recites aloud in Janazah Prayer.

There are some other du'ās which are narrated from Prophet Muhammad (ﷺ) and they can be found in Hadith Books. All of these du'ās can be said together or individually. Other du'ās can be said with these du'ās but it is better to stick to du'ās approved by Prophet (ﷺ).

ENDING THE JANAZAH PRAYER
(Fourth Takbeer)

Then the Imam should say the fourth Takbeer and the congregation should follow and after that the Imam should say "As-salāmu 'alaykum wa rahmatul-lāh" turning his face to the right first and then to the left; and the congregation should do the same.

Note:- Some people stress a lot on saying du'ās after the completion of Janazah prayer but we did not find a single hadith supporting this idea. Janazah prayer is designed so that all the du'ās a person wants to say for the deceased can be said after the third Takbeer. This was the authentic practice of Prophet Muhammad (ﷺ) and his companions.

PRAYER DURING A JOURNEY

Islam is a practical way of life and considers the situations in which its followers may face difficulties. So Allah has made the things easy for the believers in such situations. Included in these facilities is the permission for shortening and combining daily prayers during a journey.

1. QASR PRAYER (Short Prayer)

When a Muslim is on a journey he should pray 2 rakats fard for Zuhr, Asr and Isha. Fajr and maghrib prayers remain as they are.

2. IT IS MORE REWAERDFUL TO PRAY A QASR PRAYER (Short -Prayer)

It is more rewardful to pray a Qasr Prayer while on a journey. The Messenger of Allah (ﷺ) said: "It is a gift from Allah which he has bestowed upon you; so you should accept it."
(Muslim).

3. COMBINING PRAYERS

A person on a journey can combine Zuhr and Asr prayers together praying them both at Zuhr or Asr time. He can also combine Maghrib and Isha prayers together praying them both at Maghrib or Isha time.

Ibn Abbas (R.A.) said that the Messenger of Allah (ﷺ) used to combine Zuhr and Asr together when he was on a journey and also he used to combine Maghrib and Isha.

(Bukhari).

Mu'āz (R.A.) said that the Messenger of Allah (ﷺ) was on a journey for the Battle of Tabook. If the sun had already declined when he wanted to start his journey after having camped somewhere, he would combine his Zuhr and Asr prayers together and pray them both at Zuhr time, and if he decided to move before the sun had declined then he delayed the Zuhr prayer and prayed it combined with Asr prayer at Asr time. And if the sun had already set when he wanted to move he would combine Maghrib and Isha together at Maghrib time. And if the sun had not set when he wanted to move he would delay Maghrib and pray it with Isha at Isha time.

(Abu Dawūd, Tirmizi).

These hadiths are very clear in their meaning and prove that combining prayers while on a journey is a proved and a regular practice of Prophet Muhammad (ﷺ). Still, there are people who do not believe in combining prayers together while they are travelling. However, this is a gift from Allah which the believers should accept gratefully and if someone wants to reject Allah's and his Messenger's offer it is up to him.

4. WHEN TO SHORTEN AND COMBINE PRAYERS

Now, there is the question as to what is the limiting distance and the duration of the journey to make the facility of Qasr and Jama valid.

a. Yahya bin Yazeed said, "I asked Anas bin Malik (R.A.) when the Qasr prayer was allowed?" Anas (R.A.) answered that the Messenger of Allah (ﷺ) whenever he went away about 3 miles he prayed Qasr.

(Muslim, Ahmad, Abu Dawūd, Baihaqi).

b. Abu Sa'eed (R.A.) said that whenever Rasulullah (ﷺ) travelled about 1 farsakh, approximately 3 miles, he would pray Qasr.

(Talkhees Ibn Hajr).

On the basis of these hadiths a person can pray Qasr and can combine prayers when the distance he travels away from home is 3 miles. This distance is the minimum limit for Qasr prayer. However, there are many varied opinions on the minimum limit of the distance; for example 9 miles, 48 miles or one day's journey, etc.

In our opinion the correct definition of a journey is what the society as a whole recognizes under their circumstances, the minimum limit being 3 miles.

5. DURATION OF JOURNEY

A person can pray Qasr and combine his prayers for as long as he remains on a journey, whether it takes weeks, months or years. Even if he stays put in one place to fulfil the purpose of his journey he can continue to pray Qasr and combine his prayers. However, if he intended to stay in a place for a fixed number of days then the opinions differ on how long he can go on combining and shortening his prayers, e.g. 4 days, 10 days, 17 days, 18 days, etc.

After a careful study of hadiths we can say that when someone stays in a fixed place temporarily he would be considered a traveller on a journey, and there is no limit on the number of days he can pray Qasr and combine his prayers.

6. NAFL PRAYER ON A JOURNEY

Prophet Muhammad (ﷺ) always offered Witr prayer during his journey and he emphasized and expressed the importance of 2 rakats sunnat of the Fajr prayer. Therefore, the believers should pray these, while on a journey.

But what about any other nafl and sunnat prayer?

The following hadith answers this question.

Hafs bin Asim said, "I accompanied Abdullah bin Umar (R.A.) on a journey to Makkah. On the way to Makkah he led us in the Zuhr prayer and offered 2 rakats. Then he went to sit in his tent. He saw some people praying and asked me what they were doing.

'They are praying nafl,' said I. Then he said, 'If I could pray nafl then I should have prayed the complete fard prayer.' Then he continued, 'I accompanied the Messenger of Allah (ﷺ) on a journey. He did not pray during his travels more than 2 rakats. Then I accompanied Abu Bakr (R.A.), Umar (R.A.), and Uthman (R.A.) and they did the same as Prophet Muhammad (ﷺ).' There is a good example for you in the practice of Prophet ﷺ
"(Bukhari).

There are some other hadiths which prove that some of the companions used to pray nafls during their journey. It is better not to pray nafls while travelling but if you stay somewhere and have time you may do so.

How to perform Prayers

Prayers begin with the intention to perform them. Intention should not be expressed in words, for its place is in the heart.

1 The worshipper should face the Qibla (Niche) with the inward resolve to perform the prayers. Then he has to raise his hands on both sides of the face saying "Allahu Akbar."

2 Then he should put the right hand on the left one and recite the Fatiha and a short Chapter of the Quràn, or some of its verses.

3 The hands are again to be raised on both sides of the face and the words "Allahu Akbar" should be uttered as the worshipper prepares to bow.

4 The bow should be from the hips, so that the back would be in straight horizontal posture. The hands are placed, fingers spread on the knees and upper parts of the legs. The worshipper silently repeats three times "Glory be to my Lord, the Great."

5 When he straightens himself up after the bow, he should again raise his hands on both sides of the face and say "Allah listens to whoever thanks Him" followed by "Our Lord, thanks be to Thee."

6 Saying "Allahu Akbar", the worshipper genuflects, bending his knees before his hands

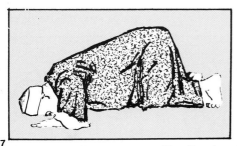

7 Then the worshipper prostrates himself twice, with his nose and forehead placed on the ground between the palms of his hands.

8 While prostrating himself in prayer, the worshipper should straddle his hands and thighs, pointing the fingers and toes towards the Qibla. The worshipper repeats three times "Glory be to my Lord, the Highest."

9 Between the two prostrations, the worshipper should sit upright, saying "Allahu Akbar", putting his hands on his thighs near the knees.

10

When seated to recite Al-Tashahud (testimony), the worshipper, in the first sitting, should sit with the right foot upright and the left foot flat under him. In the second sitting of the final raka'a, he should put his left foot under his right leg, sitting on the latter and supporting himself on his bottom. This posture is known as 'Tawarrok'. During the recital of Al-Tashahud, when the worshipper says "I bear witness that there is no God except Allah", he should raise the forefinger of his right hand.

11
Then the worshipper should turn his head to the right, until his right cheek-bone may be seen, and say "assalamu alaikum wa rahmatullah."

12

He should then turn his head to the left, until his left cheek-bone may be seen, and say again "assalamu alaikum wa rahmatullah."